Walk!

the

Costa Blanca

Mountains

with

Charles Davis

DISCOVERY WALKING GUIDES LTD

*For Jeannette and the
Hand of Fatima.*

Walk! The Costa Blanca Mountains
First Edition - April 2012

Copyright © 2012

Published by
Discovery Walking Guides Ltd
10 Tennyson Close, Northampton NN5 7HJ, England

Maps
Maps are adapted from Costa Blanca Mountains Tour &
Trail Map published by **Discovery Walking Guides
Ltd**

Photographs
All photographs in this book were supplied by the
author.

Front Cover Photographs

Castell de Castells: Cumbre
de Aixort (Walk 18)

Walk 34, Vall de Laguar, Cavall Verd

Walk 15 (Famorca - Little Wolf)   Puig Campana (Walk 3)

ISBN 9781904946854

Text and photographs* © Charles Davis

Walk!
the
Costa Blanca Mountains

CONTENTS

Contents   5
The Author   9

INTRODUCTION: Climbing Into Cliché; a Better Costa Blanca   10

Using GPS in the Costa Blanca   20
Symbols Rating Guide   21

Map Information
     Location Maps   22
     Map Notes & Legend   24

THE WALKS

SIERRAS

1   Xalo: PR7 Serra de Bernia   26
     3 walker, 2½ hours, 7.95 km, ascents & descents
     260 metres, 5 refreshments (circular)

2   Polop: Monte Ponoig   29
     5 walker, 4 hours, 9.26 km, ascents & descents
     767 metres, 0 refreshments (linear)

3   Finestrat: Puig Campana   32
     5 walker, 4¼ hours, 10.1 km, ascents & descents
     1021 metres, refreshments 0, vertigo warning (circular)

4   Finestrat: Barranc de Sacarest   36
     3 walker, 3 hours, 10.2 km, ascents & descents
     544 metres, refreshments 0 (circular)

5   Sella: SL112 La Ruta del Aigua   40
     1 walker, 1¾ hours, 6.23 km, ascents & descents
     200 metres, refreshments 4 (circular)

6   Sella: Barrancs del Xarquer and Arc   43
     3 walker, 3½ hours, 13 km, ascents & descents
     400 metres, refreshments 2 (circular)

7   Confrides: Castell de Confrides   **46**
2 walker, 1 hour 5 mins, 3.2 km, ascents & descents
130 metres, refreshments 0 (linear or circular)

8   Confrides: Cumbre de Aitana from Font de l'Arbre   **48**
4 walker, 3 hours 5 mins, 11 km, ascents & descents
450 metres, refreshments 4 (circular)

9   Benifato: Cumbre de Aitana from Font de Partagat   **51**
3 walker, 3 hours 10 mins, 10 km, ascents & descents
450 metres, refreshments 0 (circular)

10   Benimantell: Penyo Mulero   **54**
4 walker, 2 hours 50', 10.73 km, ascents & descents
500 metres, refreshments 0 (circular)

11   Benimantell: Barrancs del Salt, Xarquer & Arc   **57**
5 walker, 3½ hours, 12.6 km, ascents & descents
500 metres, refreshments 2 (circular)

12   Benasu: El Recingle Alt   **61**
3 walker, 2½ hours, 11.5km km, ascents & descents
500 metres, refreshments 0 (linear)

13   Quatredonteda: Els Frares   **64**
(a) via Cami del Carrascal
3 walker, 51 minutes one-way, 2.16 km one-way, ascents
& descents 344 metres, refreshments 3 (linear)

(b) via Cami des Clots
3 walker, 2 hours 25 minutes, 6 km, ascents & descents
374 metres, refreshments 3 (linear)

14   Fageca: PR182 Pla de la Casa
Plus alternative access from the south   **68**
4 walker, 4 hours 40 minutes, 9.33 km, ascents & descents
563 metres, refreshments 0 (circular)

15   Famorca: Little Wolf - Mallada del Llop   **73**
3 walker, 3½ hours, 7.5 km, ascents & descents
580 metres, refreshments 3 (linear)

16   Famorca: Big Wolf - Barranc de la Canal,
Mallada del Llop, El Regall   **76**
4 walker, 4 hours 20 minutes, 10.3 km, ascents &
descents 660 metres, refreshments 3 (circular)

17   Castell de Castells: PR149 El Castellet   **80**
3 walker, 2¾ hours, 8.5 km, ascents & descents
536 metres, refreshments 4 (circular)

18   Castell de Castells: Cumbre de Aixorta and Els Arcs   **83**
4 walker, 5½ hours, 20.75 km, ascents & descents
845 metres, refreshments 4 (circular)

19   Tarbena: PR145 Parelles and Serrals via Font dels Olbis   **88**
4 walker, 3½ hours, 13.45 km, ascents & descents
450 metres, refreshments 3 (circular)

20   Bolulla: Tour of Raco Roig   **92**
2 walker, 2½ hours, 7.37 km, ascents & descents
250 metres, refreshments 0 (circular)

21   Orxa: Serra La Safor and Raco del Duc   **95**
5 walker, 6 hours 20 minutes, 18.4 km, ascents & descents
730 metres, refreshments 0 (circular)

22   Orxa: Cim de la Safor   **101**
2 walker, 1 ¾ hours, 6.28 km, ascents & descents
317 metres, refreshments 0 (linear)

LES VALLS

23   Vall de Planes: Barranc de l'Encantada   **103**
1 walker, 40 minutes one-way, 2.3 km one-way,
ascents & descents 100 metres, refreshments 0 (linear)

24   Vall de Gallinera (Benissili): Castillo de Benissili   **105**
3 walker, 1 hour 50 minutes, 6.3 km, ascents &
descents 315 metres, refreshments 0 (circular)

25   Vall de Gallinera (Benissiva): La Forada   **108**

     Linear: 3 walker, 1 hour one-way, 2.5 km one-way,
                ascents & descents 224 metres, refreshments 3

     Circuit: 3 walker, 2 hours 40 minutes, 10.5 km, ascents
                & descents 300 metres, refreshments 3

26   Pego: Refugio de la Figuereta   **111**
4 walker, 2 hours 10 minutes, 7.35 km, ascents &
descents 444 metres, refreshments 4 (circular)

27   Vall d'Alcala: Alcala de la Jovada to Es Pouet   **114**
3 walker, 3 hours 20 minutes, 15.3 km, ascents &
descents 340 metres, refreshments 3 (circular)

28   Vall d'Ebo: Travessia del Masset   **117**
2 walker, 1 hour 20 minutes, 4.62 km, ascents &
descents 207 metres, refreshments 3 (circular)

29   Tormos: Sender dels Pintors   **119**
3 walker, 2 hours 10 minutes, 3.75 km, ascents &
descents 296 metres, refreshments 3 (circular)

30   Tormos: Sender dels Poets   **121**
3 walker, 2¾ hours, 8.55 kilometres, ascents &
descents 380 metres, refreshments 3 (linear)

31   Vall de Laguar (Fleix): PR147 La Catedral del Senderisme **124**
5 walker, 3 hours 50 minutes, 13.5 km, ascents &
descents 845 metres, refreshments 3 (circular)

32   Vall de Laguar (Fleix): Barranc dels Racons   **127**
3 walker, 3 hours 40 minutes, 11.5 km, ascents &
descents 447 metres, refreshments 3 (circular)

33   Vall de Laguar (Campell):
Presa d'Isbert & Barranc del Moro   **129**
2 walker, 2 hours, 5.2 km, ascents & descents 285 metres,
refreshments 5 (circular)

34   Vall de Laguar (Campell): Cavall Verd
- the conventional circuit   **132**
3 walker, 2 hours 35 minutes, 7.6 km, ascents &
descents 315 metres, refreshments 5 (circular)

35   Vall de Laguar (Benimaurell): Cavall Verd
- the western loop   **135**
3 walker, 2 hours 5 minutes, 6.57 km, ascents &
descents 246 metres, refreshments 5 (circular)

36   Vall de Pop (Parcent): PR158 Sender de Parcent   **138**
5 walker, 4¼ hours, 14.12 km, ascents & descents 700
metres, refreshments 5 (circular)

37   Vall de Pop (Pla de Petracos):
Serra l'Alfaro and Barranc de Malafi   **142**
4 walker, 6 hours, 20.5 km, ascents & descents 530
metres, refreshments 0 (circular)

Glossary   **146**
Appendices
A **Websites**   **148**
B **Cycling**   **152**
C **Publications**   **153**

Place Names Index   **154**

Charles Davis was born in London, and has lived and worked in the United States, Sudan, Turkey, Ivory Coast, Spain and France. With the onset of middle age, he realised that the urge to roam was better satisfied by walking than bouncing about on the back of a lorry in the middle of the desert, and now divides his time between mountain tops, desk-tops and laptops. He is the author of numerous highly praised and wholly unpublished novels.

Jeanette Tallegas has spent thirty odd years labouring for the French education system, from which she has finally, gleefully, taken early retirement. Asked what she intends doing now, she resolutely replies, "Nothing". Nonetheless, she does follow the author up various gruelling mountains, frequently alarming younger adventurers who seem to assume that remote and inaccessible places are the preserve of youth.

Charles Davis is also author of the following (Discovery Walking Guides Ltd):-

Walk! The Lake District South
ISBN 9781904946168

Walk! The Alpujarras
ISBN 9781904946236

Walk! Dorset
ISBN 9781904946205

Walk! Brittany (North)
ISBN 9781904946359

GR221 Mallorca's Dry Stone Way
ISBN 9781904946489

Bumping About Brittany
ISBN 9781904946441

Walk! Mallorca North & Mountains
ISBN 9781904946496

Walk! La Gomera
ISBN 9781899554904

Walk! Mallorca West
ISBN 9781904946700

Walk! La Palma
ISBN 9781904946687

Walk! The Axarquia
ISBN 9781904946656

Walk! Andorra
ISBN 9781904946045

- and also

Walk On, Bright Boy   ISBN 9781579621537 (Permanent Press)
Walking The Dog   ISBN 9781579621674 (Permanent Press)
Costa del Sol Walks   ISBN 9788489954397 (Santana)
Costa Blanca Walks   ISBN 9788489954571 (Santana)
Standing At The Crossroads   ISBN9781579622138 (Permanent Press)

CLIMBING INTO CLICHÉ: A BETTER COSTA BLANCA

Read any good life, back to basics, season in the sun farm yarn about expats settling in Spain, and you can be fairly sure there will come a moment when the narrator takes to the mountains for a walk that proves to be a 'state of the heart' experience in which engagement with the landscape aspires to a quasi-spiritual empathy. It's a rite of passage, as vital to the format as encountering the crafty peasant with a heart of gold, having an amusing mishap with the domestic livestock, being duffed up by the elements, and displaying a comic ineptitude when confronted with the sort of quotidian challenges that generations of illiterate country dwellers have prevailed over with apparent insouciance.

Such clichés exist for a reason and it's not simply because they happen to sell books. Like all clichés, they come of observable truths. Settle in Spain and you probably will bump into the wily old boy with a winning glint in his eye, be confronted by a belligerent chicken or rogue pig, and be battered about a bit by the big weather. For the most part, these experiences are the preserve of those who uproot themselves to settle in foreign parts. But the mountains, they are something else.

Spain is defined by mountains. It is the second most mountainous country in Europe (even the famously flat bits in the middle are riven by mountains in reverse, in the form of fabulous canyons and ravines) and, though the tourist brochures may peddle images of beaches so drenched with sun that the bodies draped across them begin to resemble something being barbecued, the country's true aficionados know that this is a bit like defining a wine by the bottle or suggesting a meal is summed up by the scalloping round the edge of the plate. The substance lies elsewhere and anyone who goes to Spain simply in order to spend their time sizzling on the beach has rather missed the point.

Barranc de Malafi (Walk 37)

Good news then that the pre-eminent 'rite of passage' enjoyed by expatriate good-lifers is the one experience readily available to more transient visitors. Take a trip to Spain, be it ever so short, and you can be fairly sure that

Cavall Verd (Walk 34)

there is a great mountain experience waiting for you just round the corner, one that will take you out of yourself and bring you into a landscape that would have reduced the Romantics to paroxysms of verse making.

Nowhere is this more true than the Costa Blanca.

The beaches of Benidorm may have come to define a certain type of tourism, but just behind the coast there is a mountain-scape that rivals Mallorca as a winter walking destination, one that is part of the **Baetic Cordillera** which stretches from Andalusia to the Balearics, a playground of crags, cliffs, crests, ridges, gullies, gorges, pinnacles, peaks and over a hundred waymarked walking itineraries, and all this a mere two hours from Britain on a flight that will cost about the same as a couple of bottles of single malt. I can't promise cunning locals, obdurate donkeys, or an amusing incident with an olive press. Those parts of the formula are generally a consequence of upping sticks and settling elsewhere. But I can guarantee some great walking that will take you into the heart of the country like nothing else. Who knows, you may even end up changing life.

Take a cursory glance at the mountains behind the Costa Blanca and, even by Spanish standards, they can present a dry, austere, almost intimidating aspect that is curiously at odds with the better forested regions of the other Baetic ranges

This is, for instance, the only area I know where local maps actually mark the location of solitary 'monumental' trees, most of them named, and most looking pretty modest to Northern European eyes. But behind their harsh facade, the summits, ridges and ravines of which this unique landscape is composed are utterly enchanting and, the more you get into them, the more beguiling they become, their rugged grandeur, sumptuous vistas, and secret corners exercising an insidious charm that is sure to have you coming back for more.

Els Arcs (Walk 18)

Like most of the northern belt of the **Baetic Cordillera**, the mountain ranges in Alicante Province are largely composed of limestone, the solubility of which gives the sierras their characteristic 'serrated' aspect (**sierra** being Spanish for saw), guarantees a fair amount of karst underfoot, and furnishes several walks with their objective in the shape of the natural arches or windows that appear in the weathered rock, variously known as *arcs*, *forats*, and *finestras*.

Apart from the diminutive 'monumental' trees, the classic vegetation is holm oak scrub (get one of the small sharp leaves in your boot and you'll rapidly understand why

Genista (Spanish broom)

Antirrinhum hispanicum

it's also called holly oak) interwoven with heather, broom, thyme, and cistus, patched with the odd splash of frothy young pine, and speckled with some delightful wild flowers.

If you're new to the region and have yet to undergo the trick of the heart that engages one with a novel and outwardly daunting environment that can seem almost impenetrable to the casual observer, it should be said that the desiccated wildness of the mountains is deceptive.

For one thing, they may look dry, but in fact they're absolutely brimming with water.

Even toward the end of summer before the autumn rains have come, springs frequently seep onto paths, many walks visit *area recreativas* conceived around fonts, and there's scarcely a village that doesn't have its own water supply piped directly down from the nearest mountain.

Raco del Duc (Walk 21)

In our risk averse, litigious times, most fonts are plastered with signs announcing that the water is untreated or unsuited for human consumption or downright non-potable. As a rule, these warnings can be ignored with impunity, and are even expected to be ignored. On at least one itinerary featured here (Walk 36), a 'non-potable' source also has a sign saying you can't take more than 25 litres at a time! The quota may seem a bit redundant to walkers accustomed to carrying a couple of litres in their backpack, but the Spanish do love their spring water, and sooner or later you can expect to see someone rolling up to a font with a lorry-load of empties that will be patiently filled over the course of an hour or more. The line to take with Spanish spring water was perhaps best summed up for me by one old boy I met in **Llombai (Vall de Gallinera)**. Asked if the water from a local source was potable, he said, "No es potable, pero es bueno." Follow the locals and the chances are that, afterwards, even the best bottled waters will taste slightly artificial.

Despite the sheer drama of the mountains, the wildness is also illusory, for this landscape has been so heavily worked that even the most remote corners carry some imprint of mankind's industrious ingenuity. Often times, terracing appears in the most unlikely looking nooks and crannies, tessellating the rockscape with tiny lozenges of cultivated terrain that only a lunatic or someone very, very hungry indeed would contemplate farming.

At the other end of the scale, there are places where the terracing is so extensive that it looks as if, rather than reclaiming land from the mountain, they actually built the mountain itself, raising the thing up layer by layer, tier upon tier, until only the very top resembles something fashioned by nature rather than man.

terracing around Sella, Walks 5 & 6

Many terraces have been abandoned and the decline of a foraging culture that cleared the woods of scrub and kindling has resulted in increasingly frequent forest fires over the course of the last century, but traditional crops remain a vital part of the local economy. Olives are still harvested, either by picking, beating or simply laying nets below the trees and waiting for the fruit to drop, and new trees are being planted, even new terraces being carved out of the mountain, in response to campaigns promoting the Mediterranean diet.

Parcent (Walk 36)

Almond and cherry orchards are abundant, the villages in the valleys are ringed with citrus groves and allotments so alluring that they nearly had me hopping over the fence, and there are some excellent local wines that wouldn't necessarily excite your more refined palate, but do the trick for anyone who wants 'a good basic red'.

Staying in the *vall* of the same name, I was delighted to discover that I could get mildly drunk each night and still claim I was drinking 'Pop'. In fact, come to think of it, these mountains are a dipsomaniac vegetarian's dream.

The other significant human activity, more localized but no less striking in its impact on the landscape, is war. The Costa Blanca mountains are indelibly marked by the Moors. Place names prefixed with 'Beni', 'Bini', or 'Al' are frequent and many villages hold annual festivals of 'Moros y Cristianos'. It is, of course, the expulsion of the Moors that the festivals celebrate rather than the consanguinity of cultures, but though the xenophobia to which the Christianized Moriscos were subsequently subjected was meant to promote the *pureza* of the Spanish peoples, one only has to look at the facial features of the locals to see how

multi-culturalism Spanish style

successful that sorry idea was.

Nonetheless, the most manifest traces of the Moorish past are not to be found in toponymy, fiestas, or genetics, but in the castles they built in a vain attempt to hold back the all conquering Catalan hero, Jaume I. Naturally, these prick rather than blanket the landscape, but they are so spectacular that, for my money, they are an essential part of the Costa Blanca experience.

Curiously, for a region so dependent on tourism, most of these fortifications are neglected. They are uniformly lovely places, invariably perched on vertiginous eyries, surrounded by wild mountain-scapes and extraordinary views, and are about as evocative as your most ardent lover of old stones could wish. Yet they are never signposted, rarely touched upon by official paths, and rely upon people like me nosing about to bring them to the casual visitor's attention. I can only suppose the authorities haven't the wherewithal to maintain them and don't want to be liable if some hapless tourist gets coshed by a bit of falling masonry, an eventuality, I hasten to add, that is hardly likely if you don't do anything foolish like dancing about on crumbling battlements.

The Waymarked Paths

PR signpost, Walk 11

There are some 6,000 kilometres of waymarked paths in the Comunitat Valenciana, of which Alicante province and the Costa Blanca mountains are a part, 4000 of them in the yellow and white waymarked PR network of *Pequeños Recorridos* i.e. 'short' walks of between 10 and 50 kilometres as opposed to the LDP GRs.

This sounds pretty impressive and some of the PRs are superb, but they are very far from representing the best possible walks.

PR cross (Walk 22)

The first drawback is a question of consistency. PR path makers seem to fluctuate between two extremes, on the one hand getting into their cars and splashing a bit of paint about on the local minor (and sometimes not so minor) roads, on the other, designating though not always waymarking the most improbable, precipitous, and imperceptible goat tracks they can find, some of which are so exiguous that they bear the same relationship to your average path as a Brazilian bikini does to a nineteenth century bathing suit.

Moreover, the majority of these itineraries have a distressing tendency to trace out long, linear routes between distant places perfectly devoid of any mutual public transport link, which is all very well when you're walking, but means you're a bit stumped at the end of the day when you find yourself thirty kilometres from your car, are beginning to flag a little, and wouldn't mind going home for a glass of pop.

A third shortcoming is that, Brazilian bikini jobs notwithstanding, like most official itineraries, PRs are generally allergic to wild walking, cleaving instead to irreproachably safe dirt tracks. This is understandable, but often results in an exacerbation of the 'splash a bit of paint about on the local roads' tendency. As indicated above, people still do work in these mountains and, naturally enough, your average farmer would prefer to drive to work on asphalt or concrete rather than wrecking his tyres and clutch on rough dirt tracks that wash away every year. So the town hall obliges and tracks that once constituted decent walking routes become rather tedious tarmac lanes.

SL fingerpost (Walk 28)

Another network that has been developed in recent years is that of the green and white waymarked SLs or Senderos Locales, shorter itineraries of less than 10 kilometres. These are poorly promoted and, often as not, the first you'll know of an SL is when you turn up in a village and find a hazy aerial photograph with a few dots scattered about and a vague line sketched on it. And that'll be your lot apart from the odd signpost, often as not tucked out of sight, well away from the start of the walk. This is a pity as the general concept is a good one.

Despite these weaknesses, the official itineraries are a useful starting point for developing decent walks. With a little massaging most PRs can be manipulated into something rather fine (which is what we aim to do in this book), given time the SLs should become an attractive alternative to the more arduous walks dictated by the region's topography, and the work done by local authorities is to be commended.

Some of the official routes are fabulous, several town halls have gone to great pains to restore old transhumance trails and traditional paved paths, and any effort to encourage people out into the countryside has got to be laudable. But it's worth bearing in mind that, just because something has a signpost on it, it doesn't necessarily mean it's either

unofficial waymark (Walk 20)

desirable or practical.

You will also see unofficial waymarks, sometimes mimicking the yellow and white PR stripes, but generally taking the form of bright dots or stylized arrows. Needless to say, these have no consistency whatsoever, since they are not standardized, but they are worth looking out for because they are generally done by local enthusiasts, and will usually take you to places that are far more interesting than those visited by the PRs. True, they might not always take you out again, but that's a different matter.

Potential Problems

Subject to the provisos stipulated in the introductions to specific itineraries, walking in the Costa Blanca mountains is rarely dangerous. As with any mountain escapade, you have to take account of the elements, and anyone who sets off for a walk in hot weather without sufficient water is asking for trouble.

on Walk 27

Despite my championing of the region's springs, it would be foolish to rely upon these exclusively, so even if there is a font en route, take some water with you just in case. That aside, there are two potential problems worth mentioning.

Bear in mind that the hunting fraternity is

Walk 10

not always composed of men (and they always are men - why don't women want to go out killing stuff?) of the most delicate disposition and they are not necessarily delirious with joy to find foreigners tramping about places where they are accustomed to blasting away with impunity.

I'm not saying they're going to shoot you on purpose or anything. Or even that they will perforce be unfriendly. Most are perfectly decent people and a few words of Spanish usually work wonders, but if you have the choice, you may wish to think twice before walking on

watch out for hunters

Thursdays and the weekends (especially Sunday) during the hunting season.

The season varies slightly according to local bylaws, but basically runs from mid October until December for small game and into February for wild boar.

If you are going to walk on those days, the nearer the coast and the further from the hinterland the better. As a rough guide, the following walks will not necessarily be hunter free, but are at least susceptible to being walker tolerant if only, in some instances, because there are more of us than them: 1- 6; 11 & 12; 17; 24-26; 31-35.

Walk 31

Though making it up as you go along is one of the great pleasures of walking in wild terrain, some prudence is advisable on the Costa Blanca, as many paths have been abandoned and are hazardous as a result. We, for instance, did one longish walk from **Benigembla** up to **Alts del Cocoll** which, magnificent scenery notwithstanding, didn't make it into the book because the paths are in such poor shape that it was all really rather disagreeable.

Worse, when we returned to the village an old woman told us (a little too gleefully for my tastes) that an Englishmen had disappeared on this route a few years back and his body hadn't been found for nine months, despite the best efforts of a British army search and rescue team.

Likewise, treat with caution publications depicting paths that have not been recorded with a GPS. Some of the maps I saw when researching this book looked absolutely beautiful until I tried to relate them to the lay of the land, whereupon entire days were lost attempting to conjure out of the brush paths that no longer exist or possibly never existed at all.

The Walk! Book

The walks are roughly organized into the sierras of **Marina Baix**, **Comtat** and **Safor**, and the area known as **Les Valls of Marina Alt**. If you're new to the region, basically this means that, if you divide the Tour & Trail map into four quarters, **Les Valls** is the top right hand quarter, the rest the sierras. However, when it seemed more logical, I have breached this rule.

For instance, walks from **Castell de Castells**, which is normally considered part of the **Vall de Pop**, are classified under sierras, because that is what they excel at. By contrast, **Tormos** isn't in a valley at all, but since the **Serra del Migdia** helps define two of the best known **Valls**, it's included in that section of the book.

The walks are numbered clockwise beginning from **Bernia**, though I've headed back east halfway round and listed walks in the **Serra de Aixorta** before moving on to the northern *sierras*.

The featured **sierras** are as follows: **Bernia** (Walk 1), **Polop** (24), **Aitana** (5-11), **Serrella** (12 - 17), **Aixorta** (18&20), and **Safor** (21&22). *Sierras* included in the 'Valls' section are **La Forada** (25), **Migdia** (29&30), **Carrascal de Parcent** (36) and **Alfar**o (37). The valleys are the **Valls de Planes** (23), **Gallinera** (24&25), **Alcala** (27), **Ebo** (28), **Laguar** (31-35), and **Pop** (37).

See the contents list at the start of the book, location maps, and access details within each itinerary for more precise locations of all walks.

When a walk follows a PR or SL in its entirety or with only minor deviations, the number of the PR/SL appears in the title. Otherwise, sections coinciding with waymarked itineraries are identified within the body of the text.

Looking south from Bernia, Walk 1

Most walks are circular, reflecting not so much the nature of the terrain as a personal prejudice against going back the same way or messing about with buses. Where appropriate, short versions are usually linear walks to an interesting spot en route.

on Walks 14 & 16

Unless otherwise specified, refreshment ratings are premised entirely on location, a high rating going to restaurants that are uncommonly remote or so perfectly placed en route that it would almost be a crime not to patronize them. If you're picnicking, it's worth checking

Castell de Confrides (Walk 7)

out local bakers and butchers, the former for Mallorcan style pizzas and pasties (*coca* and *empandillas*), the latter for the region's excellent charcuterie. The butcher in Confrides is particularly recommended and I spotted a dry tenderloin in **Castell de Castells** that I still regret not buying.

You will find a mix of Spanish and Catalan terms in the text. As a general rule, I've used the language found on signs on the spot, which is usually Catalan. However, some words may appear in Spanish out of force of habit, when used in a general context, or simply out of invincible ignorance.

Walk 21

Enough. You don't need me wittering on here. There's serious stuff to be done. Let's Walk!

GPS reception is generally good on all of our walking routes included in our new **Walk! the Costa Blanca Mountains**. If it's your first visit to this region, then GPS will provide you with the pinpoint navigational accuracy you can rely on while discovering these exciting and adventurous landscapes, plus helping you quickly locate the start of each walking route. The GPS waypoint files for all routes are available as free downloads from our website at:-

www.walking.demon.co.uk/pnfs.htm
www.dwgwalking.co.uk/pnfs.htm

Download the Walk! the Costa Blanca Mountains zip file, then unzip the file into its individual gpx files, then load the gpx file(s) into your GPS unit.

If you have a modern 'mapping' GPS unit such as an Adventurer or Lowrance Endura, then you can use the digital edition of **Costa Blanca Mountains Tour & Trail Map** to give you a real time mapping display showing exactly where you are on the walking route. Our Tour & Trail Maps are also available for use on your mobile phone using apps from **Viewranger**, **Memory Map** and **MyTrail**s.

All of the Walk! the Costa Blanca Mountains walking routes can be easily navigated without using GPS by following each route's detailed walk description.. However, using GPS gives you the added confidence of knowing exactly where you are on each route, especially if you are using a mapping GPS or phone equipped with the Costa Blanca Mountains Tour & Trail Map.

If you want to know about GPS and how it can help your own adventuring, or you are thinking of buying a GPS, then see our 'Choosing and Using GPS' on our website. 'GPS The Easy Way' (£4.99 for the book or free as a pdf download on our website), will give you a clear explanation of how these modern navigational aids work and can be used for your benefit:-

Ask not, "What is GPS?" Ask ,"What can GPS do for me?"

our rating for effort/exertion:-
1 very easy   **2** easy   **3** average
4 energetic   **5** strenuous

approximate **time** to complete a walk (compare your times against ours early in a walk) - does not include stopping time

approximate walking **distance** in kilometres

approximate **ascents/descents** in metres (N = negligible)

circular route

linear route

risk of **vertigo**

refreshments (may be at start or end of a route only)

Walk descriptions include:

- timing in minutes, shown as (40M)
- compass directions, shown as (NW)
- heights in metres, shown as (1355m)
- GPS waypoints, shown as (Wp.3)

WALK
LOCATOR
MAP

Please Note:
This locator map is
intended to give a
general indication
of each walk area.

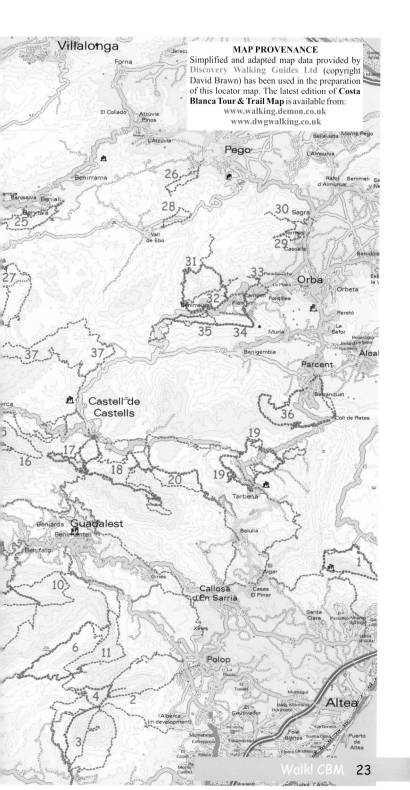

The map sections used in this book have been taken from Costa Blanca Mountains Tour & Trail Map published by Discovery Walking Guides Ltd. All map sections are aligned so that north is at the top of the page. In the interests of clarity, not all waypoints referred to in the walk descriptions are shown in the map sections. Dedicated map sections are produced for each walking route so that only the waypoints for that route are shown on the map for that route, making it easier to follow the route on the map section and to know where you are on the route.

Costa Blanca Mountains Tour & Trail Map is a 1:40,000 scale full colour map. For more information on DWG publications, write to DWG Ltd., 10 Tennyson Close, Northampton NN5 7HJ, England, or visit:

www.walking.demon.co.uk   www.dwgwalking.co.uk

Tour & Trail Map Legend

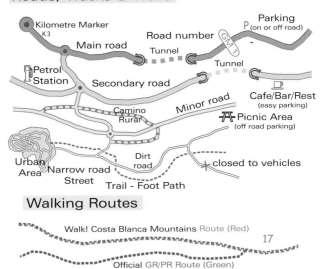

Roads, Tracks & Trails

Kilometre Marker
K 3

Main road

Road number

Parking
P (on or off road)

Tunnel

Tunnel

Petrol Station

Secondary road

Cafe/Bar/Rest
(easy parking)

Camino Rural

Minor road

Picnic Area
(off road parking)

Urban Area

Dirt road

closed to vehicles

Narrow road
Street

Trail - Foot Path

Walking Routes

Walk! Costa Blanca Mountains Route (Red)

17

Official GR/PR Route (Green)

Waypost symbols for both
GR (Gran Recorrido) and
PR (Local Recorrido) walking routes

Altitude

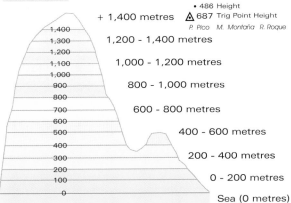

+ 1,400 metres   • 486 Height   △ 687 Trig Point Height

P. Pico   M. Montaña   R. Roque

1,200 - 1,400 metres

1,000 - 1,200 metres

800 - 1,000 metres

600 - 800 metres

400 - 600 metres

200 - 400 metres

0 - 200 metres

Sea (0 metres)

Features

≶ Mirador viewpoint   🌢 Spring   ⋒ Cave   🎋 Picnic area

🗋 Petrol   ⌷ Bar/Rest   P Parking   ℓ Information Office

⊞ Sports Ground   ⊞ Cemetery   ♰ Church   ♁ Chapel

🗲 Lighthouse   ⛫ Tower   ⛺ Camping   ⊹ Wind Turbine

🏰 Castle (ruin)   🏨 Hotel   🏠 Important House   Ⲙ Mast

🏚 Forestry House   ⊟ House   🏚 Barn

1 PR7 SERRA DE BERNIA

The Serra de Bernia is hugely popular with Costa Blanca ramblers and with good reason. It's a wonderfully wild little mountain with a very distinctive profile, outstanding in every sense, above all when viewed from the hinterland (notably on Walk 18), from where it looks like the sort of thing that only people with hard hats, hard attitudes, and lots of rope would be advised to tackle. In fact, the walking on this, the classic tour of the sierra, is relatively easy, and it only earns its exertion rating for a bit of rough ground underfoot . . . . and the crawling. Yup. The highlight of this itinerary is the **Cova del Forat**, a fifteen metre natural tunnel taking us underneath rather than over the top of the mountain. Less than a metre high at its lowest point, this is a hands and knees job that won't be to the taste of claustrophobics, but which is wonderful infantile fun for those of us who don't object to having several tons of rock over our backs. For those who do, the short version to the ruins of the sixteenth century **Fort de Bernia** is not to be missed: good paths, great views, and the remains of what is said to be the finest exemplar of Renaissance military architecture in the region.

The route is well waymarked for the most part, though beware if you're doing it in reverse. There's a rocky stretch a couple of hundred metres northwest of the tunnel. The way down is obvious, but people climbing have a tendency to end up doing just that, climbing rather than walking and it is a tendency. I met a party of English walkers who had mistaken the way. When I pointed out the easier route, one of the women wailed: 'I know, we do this EVERY time!' She didn't seem too upset by this. In fact, I think she was quite chuffed with herself. Nonetheless, if you do choose to do the circuit clockwise, when the path disappears in rough rock a couple of kilometres from the start, climb to the right of the rocks rather than going straight up.

Short Version: Fort de Bernia (Exertion 2)

Access: the walk starts from the **Cases de Bernia** on the CV749, a road that doesn't actually 'go' anywhere, but loops south between **Benissa** and **Xalo**. It is in fact two roads that have been tacked together, presumably for administrative purposes, and which meet at a T-junction between kms 12 & 13. Our itinerary starts at the large dirt parking area on the left of the **Cases de Bernia** spur, 450 metres south of the T-junction.

our start

50 metres south of the parking area, where the lane swings left, we fork right on a dirt track flanked by fingerposts and mapboards (Wp.1 0M). Apart from one brief shortcut, we follow this track until it ends. Ignoring a track branching off to the right 160 metres from the start (Wp.2), we stick with the main,

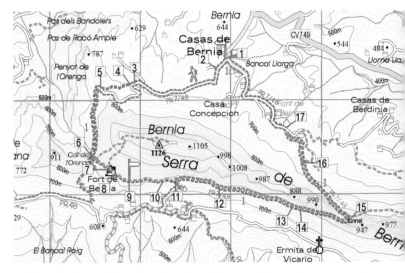

increasingly rough track, going through an equally rough gateway, after which we veer west toward the sweeping, rock-tipped spur of the **Penyot de l'Orenga** (aka **Raco de la Segaissa**). After a little over a kilometre, we pass a clear path that branches off to the left (Wp.3 16M) then fork right at a solitary pine 100 metres later, on the shortcut path, which is marked by a cairn splashed with yellow paint (Wp.4 18M).

The shortcut rejoins the track directly behind the **Penyot** (Wp.5 24M), from where we have fine views of the **Sierras de Aixorta** and **Aitana**. Bearing right, we follow the track and its continuation as a path towards the impressive crags of **Morro de la Campana**, behind which we cross the **Coll de l'Orenga** and pass a very minor path climbing toward the ridge on our left (Wp.6 41M).

Sticking to the main path and forking right at a Y-junction 100metres later (Wp.7), we cross the ruins of the **Fort de Bernia**, on the far side of which several paths splinter into the scrub, nearly all of them (not very helpfully) waymarked. Descending a couple of metres, we fork left on a reasonably broad path with a bright green waymark (Wp.8), confirmed a few metres later by PR waymarks.

Fort de Bernia

Some care required here as the people with the paint seem at odds with one another about what the **PR7** and **PR48** (which climbs from **Callosa d'en Sarria**) should do at this juncture. Look for the green waymark first THEN follow the yellow and white PR waymarks.

A good path with glorious sea views leads to a waypost (Wp.9 54M 3km), beyond which the ground gets rougher as we pass above a scattering of small houses. 400 metres after the waypost, we approach a first, fairly narrow strip of scree, just before which yellow and yellow and white waymarks down to the right (Wp.10 62M) indicate an 'easy' way (watch your step, it's off path and crosses sharp karst) onto the far side of the scree. From here to the tunnel, the clear path is regularly breached by stretches of scree, none of which pose any problems. 100 metres later, we reach a signposted junction, where the tail of the **PR7** (climbing from **Altea**) joins our route from the right (Wp.11 65M). Bearing left for the 'Forat', we continue in an easterly direction, traversing a longer stretch of scree and ignoring 'ways' climbing to the north.

Our next waystage is a large holm oak, perched in solitary splendor on a slope of thin scree (Wp.12 75M). Thereafter, the vegetation becomes richer as we approach the dramatic pinnacles at the eastern tip of the ridge, dipping up and down along the flank of the mountain, mostly on a good path, but with occasional outcrops of rock.

Wp.12 large Holm Oak

The path disappears briefly in a rockslide (Wp.13 91M), but waymarks indicate our route across the rocks to recover a clear way trodden into the scree (Wp.14 94M). This soon becomes a good dirt path, one that shows every sign of ending with a sheer drop into the sea.

It doesn't, not quite, but it's a near thing. In fact, the path climbs in easy stages, almost to the very end of the ridge, where we come to the unmistakable tunnel in the middle of the **Cova del Forat** (Wp.15 104M), at which point anyone who had their doubts will find out just how acute their claustrophobia is.

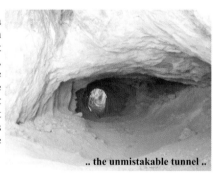

.. the unmistakable tunnel ..

There's no questioning what to do now, so it's down on our hands and knees to crawl through to the shady side of the mountain, where a clear dirt path descends (NW) to cross a well polished sheet of rock below a shallow cave this is where people climbing from the north often go astray. A few metres later, we recover the good path, which we follow for a steady, occasionally skittery descent until it joins a dirt track at the **Font de Bernia**. En route, the path splits for 50 metres (Wp.16 123M), but is otherwise unmistakable. At the font (Wp.17 130M), we simply bear left and follow the track back to the start.

2 MONTE PONOIG

Looking for the Lion

Who are the Big Beasts of Benidorm? The real Big Beasts of Benidorm are the two great mountains that dominate the skyline behind the resort, **Puig Campana** and **Monte Ponoig** (aka **Ponoch**), the latter of which even has a big beast nickname, The Sleeping Lion. Personally, I can't say I actually see the resemblance.

What I can tell you is that the comparison with something large, wild and beautiful is entirely appropriate, for **Monte Ponoig** is nothing but large, wild and beautiful.

Our take on this fine mountain is a piece of shameless cherry picking, extracting the best bits of the **PR**s **16** & **17** (the latter a variant, unmapped elsewhere as far as I know) while studiously ignoring the road walking that frames the full itineraries. Though a linear route, I don't think anyone will be complaining about doing the same path twice, for the views are fabulous in both directions. Pathfinding is never a problem, though given the steep climb at the start, path following sometimes is. The path is well made all the way to Wp.5, good until Wp.6, and only for the last 400 metres is some care required, first in following the waymarks and cairns during the ascent, second in picking your way over the loose stones on the descent. The route is designated 'El Cigarri' on wayposts, after the pass at the head of the **Barranc de la Canal**. For a slightly easier approach to **Monte Ponoig** see Walk 4.

Access: the walk starts above the village of **Polop**, which straddles the CV70 between **Benidorm** and **Alcoi**. From the southern end of the black railed bridge over the *rambla* on the C3318 (effectively a bypass separating the old village from new housing developments), we take the road climbing towards the unmistakable rise of **Ponoig**. This is the **Cami Runar**, the sign of which is not clearly visible from the main road. However, we immediately turn right into the **Avenida de la Constitucio**, which climbs into the **Urbanizacion La Paz**. If you're arriving from the coast, look out for the **Maxi Dias** supermarket on your left as you approach **Polop**, shortly after which you'll pass the village limits sign. The **Cami Runar** is the second on the left, a little under 150 metres later, immediately before the bridge. If you're approaching from inland, the turning is immediately on the right after the bridge, which is a couple of hundred metres after the roundabout intersection of the C3318 from **Callosa d'en Sarria** and the AP1704 from **Guadalest/Benimantell**.

Once on the **Avenida de la Constitucio**, it's pretty much a question of following your nose. The *avenida* narrows as it passes under the CV70 then

Wp.1

climbs amid the newly laid roads of the *urbanizacion* to a roundabout 800 metres later, where we carry straight on. After another 200 metres, we turn right on the **Cami del Flare**, which is initially a broad *urbanizacion* road but promptly narrows (at a notional roundabout, as yet invisible apart from the roundabout sign itself) to a single track lane climbing to its termination in a large car park beside a helipad and green concrete reservoir at the foot of the **Ponoig** massif, 1.7km from the **Polop** bridge. At the near end of the car park, there is an information board about a 'Via Ferrata'; don't panic, that's not our route!

Directly to the left of the Via Ferrata information board (Wp.1 0M), a narrow path picked out with yellow and white PR waymarks climbs alongside the fence on the right of the reservoir and that's all you really need to know for the next 3.5km, as there is no way of straying off trail and it's simply a question of expending a little energy. Well, quite a lot of energy actually. In any case, stash the book, enjoy and endure.

The path climbs amid healthy pine on the southern flank of the **Barranc de la Canal**, running parallel to a track in the bed of the ravine for the first few hundred metres. Climbing steadily (very steadily), we are accompanied throughout by the looming and most unfeline cliffs of **Ponoig**. The gradient eases briefly after a little over 400 metres and the **Cigarri** pass comes into view at the top of the *barranc*, but the steady slog soon resumes. A little over 800 metres from the start, our path swings away from the central line of the ravine, tracing out a zig and a zag around a couple of pine-clad terraces. After veering back toward the watercourse, just opposite another patch of terracing, we climb steeply, within sight of a couple of small corral caves at the foot of the cliffs. Finally, after 1.5km of walking, we come to our first readily identifiable waystage, a confluence of two watercourses, opposite a third corral-cave (Wp.2 42M). No rest for the walker, though, the zigzags

immediately resume, as we keep climbing to reach our next identifiable and first significant waystage, the pass we saw way down below. Prepare yourself for a revelation. As we cross rough steps on the crest of the pass (Wp.3 65M 2.2km) superb views open out toward Big Beast No.1, **Puig Campana**.

To the right of **Campana**, you can see the wooded declivity of the **Coll del Pouet**, and to the right of that, a ridge of rock distinguished by two distinct pinnacles, one with a triangular top, the other oblong. This is our next objective. The path is rougher after the pass, but clear and reasonably broad, descending briefly before following a contour line across a steep escarpment. Once again, straightforward walking with no possibility of straying off path brings us to the foot of the oblong topped pinnacle, and a signposted junction with a path doubling back to the right (Wp.4 90M).

Wp.4

Wp.5

The path carrying straight on (signposted 'Font del Moli, Finestrat PR13') leads to the **Coll del Pouet** (see Walks 3 & 4). To climb **Ponoig**, we take the path doubling back to the right, signposted 'PR17 & PR13 Polop El Barranc del Gulabdar'.

Immediately after the turning, there is a shortcut on the left, which, though waymarked toward the top, is best ignored. Instead, we stick with the main path, climbing NE to pass to the right of a solitary needle of rock 75 metres later, 30 metres after which, we veer left. Immediately after passing the top of the shortcut, we come to a T-junction 5 metres to the right of another signpost (Wp.5 98M) indicating a path descending (NW) to the **Collado del Llamp** (signposted 'Polop PR1316'). We turn right, heading NNE, for 'Monte Ponoch 1.8km'.

Ignoring a shortcut doubling back to the left to join the **Collado del Llamp** path 125 metres later, we maintain a northeasterly direction, climbing steadily on a narrow but good path, overlooking the **Barranc de Gulabdar**. 550 metres from the signpost, we cross an outcrop of fissile rock (Wp.6), after which the path becomes fainter, continuing its steady climb along the westerly flank of the lion. 300 metres later, the path veers right briefly, climbing directly toward a line of oak on the spine of the beast, just beyond which we come to the summit, where there's a postbox with a visitors' book (Wp.7 134M). The views, needless to say, are superb, taking in most of the major *sierras* covered by this book. We descend via the same route, taking especial care on the return to Wp.6.

Ponoig may be a Big Beast, but for all his leonine aspirations, he is basically just the sidekick to **Puig Campana**, than which none are bigger and beastlier. Looming over **Benidorm**, it is unmistakable with its campanile form and the distinctive notch of the **Tajo de Roldan** (aka **El Portell**). It is such a distinctive feature that it has been used for millennia as a mariners' landmark. Despite being one of the hardest walks in the book, this was the itinerary on which I encountered the most people, too. It's not really surprising. It is The Costa Blanca Mountain par excellence.

Though not the highest mountain in the province, **Puig Campana** provides the steepest sustained climb in the book, the ascent via the **Barranc de les Marietes** is largely off path, and it is very, very gruelling, indeed. To be perfectly honest, having done it once before, I wasn't looking forward to repeating the experience. Do I have to? Well, yes, and so do you, probably, if you want to claim an intimate acquaintance with the mountains hereabouts. But bear in mind, it's very tough, very wild, and virtually pathless for most of the ascent. Though we stray near no cliffs, the mountain's abrupt rise out of nowhere means it's very airy up on top, emptiness all around, so there is a slight risk of vertigo.

The approach to the **Barranc de les Marietes** sounds complicated, but is relatively simple on the ground. The main climb up the **Barranc de les Marietes** sounds simple, but is relatively complicated on the ground! In both instances, we just keep going up via the clearest 'way'. Those of you used to walking poles will appreciate them toward the end of the climb. Our return is via the **PR289** or Tour of Puig Campana. We've opted for the western branch for our return as it's shorter and enjoys better views. There are two summits on **Puig Campana**. The main one with the trigpoint is at 1408 metres, its neighbour to the southwest at 1406 metres. Since I mention them several times in the text, I refer to them as 08 and 06 for the sake of brevity. For an easier approach to **Puig Campana**, see Walk 4.

5 | 4H 15M | 10.1 km | 1020m / 1020m | ⚠ | ↻ | 🍴 0 🔪

Access: From km8.2 of the CV758 in the centre of **Finestrat**, we take **Av. Reverendo Maximiliano Lopez Escudero** (signed 'Font del Moli') north toward **Puig Campana**. A kilometre later, we pass the **Font del Moli** car park.

Wp.1

There's roadside parking at the start of the walk at km1.4, either just before or just after the bridge, where there are fingerposts for the **PR12** to **Sella** & **PR13** to **Polop**.

From the rough parking area on the right after the bridge (Wp.1 0M), we set off on a broad trail climbing through the pine woods to the north,

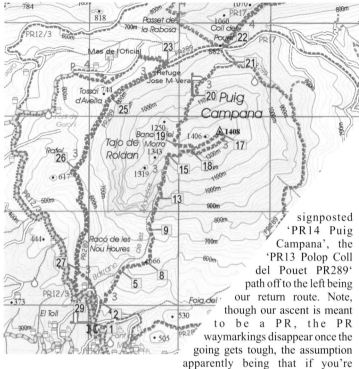

signposted 'PR14 Puig Campana', the 'PR13 Polop Coll del Pouet PR289' path off to the left being our return route. Note, though our ascent is meant to be a PR, the PR waymarkings disappear once the going gets tough, the assumption apparently being that if you're capable of doing it, you're capable of finding it yourself. There is a certain logic to this, but it's nice to discover that, once we're in the steeply raked *couloir* at the top of the **Barranc de les Marietes**, someone has taken the trouble to dapple it with red dots, suggesting that the entire enterprise is not quite so insane as it seems.

At a Y-junction just under 200 metres from the start (Wp.2), we fork right, and continue to climb through the woods. The trail disappears briefly in an outcrop of rock (Wp.3), but waymarks indicate our ongoing route, climbing directly over the rocks. Keep an eye out for the PR waymarks at this stage (i.e. before the waymarker gave it up as a bad job), as they're actually quite useful, guiding us across long stretches of bare rock amid the pine. When the clear path resumes, we ignore three minor branches off to the right in the space of 20 metres (Wp.4 11M), sticking with the main trail, which soon runs alongside the lower stretches of the **Barranc de les Marietes**. After passing some attractive little cave formations, we again ignore three branches off to the right (Wp.5 13M, Wp.6 17M, Wp.7).

Having steepened for a while (though it is as nothing to what awaits us later), our route levels out briefly on **La Planissa**, where we skirt a large fallen pine (Wp.8 24M), then traverse an area of scrub on an easier gradient, our direction of travel unmistakable as we head steadily toward the *couloir*'s long scar of scree. The path splinters as we traverse a stretch of terracing, but so long as we stick to the left bank (our right) of the **Barranc del les Marietes** and keep an eye out for the red waymarks, the route is never in doubt except, of course, in the opinion of the PR waymarker, who evidently tossed his can aside in disgust hereabouts and skedaddled off home.

Climbing steadily to steeply, we pass two clear paths doubling back to the right (Wp.9 35M), then fork left (Wp.10 36M), after which a maze of crisscrossing ways weaves up alongside the ravine like a tapestry of trails, before disappearing once again in scree and bare rock (Wp.11 43M). Small cairns and red waymarks guide us along the edge of the scree, climbing on bare rock and patches of path, a pattern that is to prevail for the rest of the ascent. 200 metres later, 200 very long metres, we reach a gate of rock protruding from the eastern wall of the *couloir* (Wp.12 52M), an unmistakable waystage, as it's splashed with graffiti, notably a large heart dedicated to Ana, an homage that has been there sufficiently long for Ana to have grown up and given birth to her own little tag artists by now . . . always presuming it was not an act of filial piety in the first place. In most walks, what we have done so far would already count as a very tough climb, but on this itinerary, the toughest is yet to come. Take a break!

the couloir up

For the present, the climb continues as before, directly over bare rock with the occasional patch of path, one such passing through a shady stand of holm oak (Wp.13 64M), after which a steep trodden 'way' runs along the edge of the scree. The way veers right briefly, before the waymarks brings us back to the edge of the scree (Wp.14 72M).

Cleaving to the narrow way between the scree and the scrub, we climb very steeply, still using occasional patches of path, but never straying more than five metres from the scree, which is our guiding line throughout. At length, great length, we clamber up a channel of rock on the right, at the top of which (Wp.15 107M) several trodden ways climb onto the eastern edge of the **Bancal del Morro**, the pass separating the two halves of the mountain. Following the clearest traces, we bear right on a gradient that is still steep, but much easier, climbing to a Y-junction (Wp.16 109M) from where we can see a fingerpost on the pass off to the left. *NOTE* If you find yourself climbing directly to the fingerpost, Wp.19 is 50 metres to the northeast, in which case do the loop to the top in reverse.

'Lost in Space'

Forking right, we climb across bare rock and scree (E then NE), picking up a green waymarked route, which is the main way to the summit. As you'll see, there's a whole maze of paths up here, as if the summit has been assailed by a marauding army crawling up from all sides, but sticking to the green route, we curve round to the east of the 06 summit, before veering sharp

Wp.19

left to reach the trig point on the 08 summit (Wp.17 130M 3.4km). The views are stunning. So is the sense of empty space. Directly southwest of 08, you will see another broad path running parallel to the green route and passing just below 06. Like its counterpart, this path splinters into a web of interweaving trails, but following its upper traces, we skirt the eastern and southern flanks of 06 to reach a Y-junction within 10 metres of the green route (Wp.18 139M). Forking right, we pass behind 06 onto its western flank, from where a reasonably clear path zigzags down to a large cairn on the **Bancal del Morro** (Wp.19 146M).

Turning right, we embark on what is an uncommon luxury on this route, a singular and clearly identifiable path, zigzagging down through the holm oak, fabulous views opening out over **Monte Ponoig** and **Penyo Cabal**.

Our path spirals down like a tightly coiled spring, the route never in doubt, numerous obvious and obviously undesirable shortcuts notwithstanding. Once again, everything is relative. On any other walk, this would be a wild path. After the ascent, it is simply a path, though some care is required on the more skittery stretches, and it's worth keeping an eye out for the red waymarks. After passing several information boards about the local flora, a clearly defined path traverses well-forested slopes, passing a branch accessing a snowpit or *pozo de nieve* (Wp.20 174M). 100 metres later, our path broadens to a trail with ambitions towards trackdom that descends past an intersection with the eastern loop of the PR289 (signposted 'Font de la Solsida') (Wp.21 183M) to reach a major junction of tracks and trails at the **Coll del Pouet** (Wp.22 186M).

Turning left for 'Font del Moli per Cami de la Serra', we descend along a dirt track, at the end of which, one path climbs to the left and another descends to a tin hut, the unmanned **Refuge José M. Vera** (Wp.23 194M). We carry straight on, descending to the refuge, immediately in front of which, we ignore a red waymarked path down to the right and bear left on the PR waymarked path (Wp.24). Except for one poorly waymarked junction toward the end (see Wp.28), it is virtually impossible to stray off path hereafter, but for the purposes of pacing progress, we cross a small spur behind a mini outcrop of rock known as the **Tossal d'Avella** (Wp.25 209M).

We then cross two shoulders below the **Tajo de Roldan**, from the second of which we see the outskirts of **Finestrat** (Wp.26 223M) and, up to our left, some extraordinary rocks angled in such a way that it looks like the entire mountain is about to topple over. After a couple of serpentine descents, the path levels out and follows a contour line leading to a narrow, cairn-marked path climbing to the left (Wp.27 243M). We ignore this, but fork left 20 metres later (Wp.28) on a path that descends to cross a dirt track (Wp.29 250M) 200 metres from our starting point.

The inspiration behind this loop round the **Barranc de Sacarest** was twofold. First, given the firedamage to the **PR289** Tour of **Puig Campana**, I wanted an alternative, relatively easy way into the heartland of the **Serra de Polop**, since it didn't seem fair that this glorious landscape should be the preserve of deranged souls like myself who are prepared to scramble up the **Barranc de les Marietes**. Second, I reckoned it would offer a marginally easier access to the summits of **Monte Ponoig** and **Puig Campana** for those who didn't fancy the more rigorous itineraries proposed in Walks 2 & 3.

In the event, this modest little outing turned out to be one of my favorite walks in the entire book, in large measure because of the utterly beautiful and scandalously neglected path across the **Passet de la Rabosa** (for my money, one of the prettiest paths in the entire region), but also because in terms of maximum reward for minimum effort this one is hard to beat. Doubtless it helped that we did the walk on a blustery sun bright winter's day, the skies washed clean by recent rain, the air burnished to a diamantine brillance. An outing on the M25 would look pretty appealing in such circumstances. But I don't believe it was just a trick of the light. If only for the half kilometre between **Coll del Pouet** and **Passet de la Rabosa**, the walk would justify itself several times over. Add to that matchless views over the natural enceinte of **Els Castellets**, a succession of grand summits, lovely paths throughout, and enough picture postcard vistas to keep you in chocolate box lids for a lifetime, and you will perhaps excuse my immoderate enthusiasm. For the record, *rabosa* means tattered, ragged, or frayed. I often feel a bit shabby myself and have a soft spot for the threadbare and unravelled places of this world, but this is plain slander. It's beautiful up there.

If you're using this as an 'easy' approach to **Puig Campana**, bear in mind that this is a relative definition. The climb from **Coll del Pouet** to the summit remains very tough (just not very, very, very tough like the way up **Barranc de les Marietes**) and still merits an exertion rating of 5. **Ponoig**, meanwhile, is a much easier proposition, reducing the exertion rating to 4 or even 3, always bearing in mind that the climb from Wp.20 to the summit is rough and occasionally follows an obscure 'way'. But even if these are not your objectives, even if you feel you don't need an 'easy' way into these mountains, I recommend this itinerary. One not to be missed.

NB Some maps identify Wp.20 as **Collado del Llamp** (aka **Llam**). I've always understood it to be the main pass at Wp.18, which most sources confirm, so we've stuck with that designation.

Short Version: to Wp.10 and back

Access: From km8.2 of the CV758 in the centre of **Finestrat**, we take **Avinguda Reverendo Maximiliano Lopez Escudero** (signposted 'Font del Moli') north toward **Puig Campana**, setting the odometer at zero. A kilometre later, we pass the **Font del Moli** car park, and continue along the

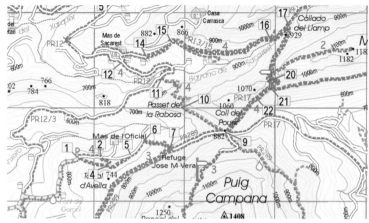

lane, which coincides with the PR12 for **Sella**. At km4.5, we turn right, then right again 200 metres later, at which point we leave the PR. We park in the large parking bay on the right at the end of the tarmac at km5.6.

Setting off from the parking bay (Wp.1 0M), we ignore a cairn-marked path climbing to the right immediately after the end of the tarmac, and continue on the **Mas de l'Oficial** dirt track. 200metres from the start, we fork right (Wp.2) on a minor track waymarked with red dots.

Els Castellets

Waypoint 5

After passing a branch down to the left onto terraces 100 metres later (Wp.3), our track dwindles to a broad trail climbing to a T-junction with a terrace path (Wp.4 9M). Turning left, still following the red waymarks, we rejoin the **Mas de l'Oficial** dirt track at a bend 300 metres later (Wp.5 14M).

We carry straight on for 200 metres, then turn right on a clearly waymarked path framed by a couple of large cairns (Wp.6 17M). This path climbs steadily and unmistakably (the occasional forks are shortcuts) to the unmanned refuge dedicated to José M Vera. As we climb, it's worth glancing over to our left at the rocky ridge fragmented with holm oak and pine. The **Passet de la Rabosa is** on the near side of the main outcrop of rock, where you should be able to pick out the silhouette of a metal sign of the type used to mark municipal boundaries and hunting reserves. Just to the right of the pass, we can also see patches of retaining wall that help define the natural line of the path from below.

At the refuge (Wp.7 31M), we join the **PR289**. Bearing left on the upper of the two paths just above the refuge, we climb to the end of a dirt track (Wp.8). Ignoring a path climbing to the right, we follow the track up to the intersection of PRs on the **Coll del Pouet** (Wp.9 40M). Directly ahead, the PR17 descends to **Polop via Taberna Margoig**. If you are using the present itinerary to approach **Puig Campana**, turn right here, then right again 200 metres later to reach the path climbing to the **Bancal del Morro** 1.8 long kilometres later (see Walk 3 Wps.16-19 for a description of the summit).

.. remarkably contorted pine ..

If you want to head directly to **Monte Ponoig**, fork left on the **PR13 Polop** trail to join Walk 2 at Wp.4 (Wp.21 of the present itinerary). Otherwise, we double back to the left on the unmarked path heading northwest. This is the bit not to be missed!

Quite why this path features in no official itineraries is beyond me. Maybe it's just too nice and the people who know the mountains wanted to keep it for themselves. It's enough to have one writing a 'Disgusted of Tonbridge' letter. The first sign that something special is up

is a remarkably contorted pine tree on our left 100 metres later.

Thereafter, we follow a contour line, descending very slightly on occasion, as superb views open out over **Els Castellets** and the sierras of the south. We then climb

Sierras of the South

Penyo Cabal

above the patches of retaining wall seen from below to the **Passet de la Rabosa** (Wp.10 49M), from where we can see the large **Mas de Sacarest** farmhouse off to the left and, on our right, **Barranc de Sacarest** and **Penyo Cabal**, the last two divided by the scar of an ancient track, used by the **PR15** and ourselves to reach the head of the ravine.

Beyond the pass, our path zigzags down (perhaps a little too far down, but then nothing's perfect) on a nicely graded descent to rejoin the PR12, which has by this stage sloughed off the tarmac of its first half dozen kilometres and become a dirt track (Wp.11 70M). Turning right, we follow the track through lovely countryside to a Y-junction directly below the **Mas de Sacarest** (Wp.12 82M). The **PR12** forks left here, passing below the house to continue towards **Sella**, but we bear right, climbing directly to the house, following waymarks for the **PR15**. Behind the **Mas**, we ignore a track off to the right leading to two wooden houses (Wp.13) and follow the PR waymarked track, which climbs to pass a fork off to the right and a wooden cabin within 30 metres of one another (Wp.14 90M), after which the track dwindles to a broad trail.

We continue climbing steadily toward the **Penyo Cabal**, bringing into view, off on our right, **Monte Ponoig**. After passing a rough track doubling back to the left (Wp.15), the gradient eases and the trail becomes so overgrown that, for long stretches, it is reduced to a path. Toward the top of the **Barranc de Sacarest**, which has been steadily deepening off to our right, we fork right at a Y-junction (Wp.16 113M). Ignoring a cairn marked path on the left 150 metres later (Wp.17 115M), we cross the **Collado de Llamp**, the broad pass between the **Barrancs de Sacarest** and **Gulabdar**, to reach a second, more distinct Y-junction (Wp.18 117M), from where we can see the **Serra de Bernia**, the **Guadalest** valley and **Callosa d'en Sarria**.

The **PR15** descends on the left over rock and brown dirt, while we fork right on an unmarked path of white grit. This is a shortcut avoiding descending to the actual junction of the **PRs15 & 17** 100 metres lower down. The path contours round the outcrop of rock on our right, fine views opening out over the **Barranc de Gulabdar** as we shadow a much broader path directly below us, the **PR17**, which we join on the far side of the outcrop of rock (Wp.19 121M). From here, we enjoy a gentle climb to the pass below **Monte Ponoig** and the signposted intersection with Walk 2 (Wp.20 131M). If you wish to climb **Monte Ponoig** at this stage, see Walk 2 Wp.5. To return to the **Coll del Pouet**, we turn left on the **Ponoig** path then immediately right on a path marked with cairns and PR waymarks. After following a contour line to the east for 150 metres, we veer round to the right and descend through a gateway of rock to another signposted junction (Wp.21 140M). Carrying straight on, we pass a minor path doubling back to the right (Wp.22) before rejoining our outward route at the **Coll del Pouet** (150M). We return to the start by the same route, with the option at Wp.4 of carrying straight on along a well trodden path leading directly back to the end of the tarmac.

The **Ruta del Aigua** in **Sella** is an object lesson in how to develop an SL. Though most of it is on surfaced lanes, it's neatly worked out, thematically coherent, well signposted and waymarked, features some useful information panels en route, and is, above all else, a charmingly bucolic stroll through a delightful domestic landscape.

It's ideal as an antidote to some of the more arduous walks in the book (we did it the day after I'd dragged myself up **Puig Campana**) or simply as a gentle outing when the weather's too hot or too cold or too wild for anything more strenuous.

In all of which, it is the antithesis of the two **Prs 198** and **199** adjacent to the village, exploring the superficially impressive **Penya de Sella**, neither of which are recommended. There is a certain 'wild man macho' appeal to scrambling up the **Runar de la Mona** on the **PR198**, but otherwise, both itineraries feature very tough climbs to reach somewhere that's almost accessible by car and, once on top, all you really get for your labours is a halfway decent view of **Aitana**, a fire ravaged landscape swathed in cistus, and a lot of aggro on obscure, often invisible paths with half the waymarks effaced. The SL, by contrast, proves the old adage that less is more.

Access: Sella lies on the CV770 north of **Villajoyosa**. From the eastern end of the village, we take the lane to the northeast, signposted 'Cementeri', 'Barranc del Arc', 'Font de l'Alcantara' (there's also a mapboard for the **PRs 9 & 12**, which follow this road), and park in the car park on the right 150 metres later. Directly above the car park, there is a line of recycling bins and a mapboard of the **PRs 198** and **199** and the **SL112**.

From the mapboard above the car park (Wp.1 0M), we follow the road on the left into the village, as indicated by an SL fingerpost. Just under 250 metres later, we take the second turning on the right (Wp.2) into *plaza major*, at the far end of which, immediately after the **Bar Casino**, we turn left (Wp.3) on the decidedly unmajor **Carrer Major**.

At the T-junction with **Calle de D Catalina** (Wp.4), we turn right then drop down to the left 75 metres later to reach the CV770 (Wp.5 11M).

Mapboard at Wp.1

Turning left on the CV770 then immediately right for **Bassa de Batle**, we descend along a surfaced path, rejoining the road 50 metres from the bridge over the **Riu de les Voltes**. At the near end of the bridge (Wp.6 14M), a nicely tailored path dips down to cross the river, beyond which we ignore a track doubling back to the right and take a surfaced lane (Wp.7) climbing south to the **Bassa de Batle** irrigation reservoir (Wp.8 20M).

At Wp.6

.. a picturesque mill-house .. (Wp.10)

Forking left for the **Assut de Salt**, we follow a narrow terrace path, passing between two houses, immediately after which we re-cross the CV770 (Wp.9 22M) onto a concrete track.

Ignoring all branches, we follow this track down to the *assut* (an Arabic word for a kind of weir, though it's generally used for a small reservoir that's little more than a walled off bend on the bank of a river), at which point the **Voltes** and **Arc** streams merge to form the **Riu Sella**. 85 metres downstream we fork left on a narrow path, climbing above a picturesque mill-house (Wp.10 33M).

Just short of an equally picturesque *caseta*, we ignore a path doubling back to the left (Wp.11 38M), and pass directly behind the *caseta*, which has an astonishingly comprehensive orchard - grapefruit, mandarins, oranges, olives, medlars, vines, they've got the lot. Joining a dirt track beyond the orchard (Wp.12 41M), we turn left and climb to a crossroads, where we turn left again, this time onto a tarmac lane (Wp.13 46M). We follow this lane for the next 1.5km, ignoring all branches, and enjoying fine views over the climbers' crags at the head of the **Riu d'Arc** valley and, off to our left, the bare flank of the **Penya de Sella**. The patch of scree in the middle of the **Penya** is the **Runar de la Mona**, the route followed by the **PR198**.

At a slanting T-junction with another lane (Wp.14 64M), we bear left down to the **Font de l'Alcantara** *area recreativa*. After visiting the spring, we continue on the lane and cross a small bridge, just beyond which a signposted path (Wp.15 70M) (coinciding with a concrete drive for the first few metres) climbs between two *casetas*. NOTE when we passed there were two very fierce dogs in the yard of the second *caseta*. They were attached and couldn't quite get to the path (God knows, they were willing!), but if you're nervous of dogs, you might prefer to follow the road up to the right after the bridge, then double back to the left on the main **Barranc del Arc** lane to rejoin the described route at Wp.16.

Joining the main **Barranc del Arc** lane directly above the casetas (Wp.16), we turn left, then double back to the right 50 metres later on a track (Wp.17 74M) passing below another *caseta*, at which point the SL briefly coincides with the **PR198**. 200 metres along the track (Wp.18 76M), we double back to the left, passing behind the *caseta* into a rough trail climbing northeast along a shallow spur. The trail climbs past a rather weary looking almond grove and into a pine wood, toward the top of which, we reach another lane (Wp.19 86M), at which point the SL and PR diverge. The PR forks right and starts getting shirty with a really wild ascent up to the **Penya de Sella**. We, meanwhile, neatly skive off, turning left on the lane, which we follow all the way back to **Sella**, where it rejoins the **Barranc del Arc** lane just above the car park.

6 BARRANCS DEL XARQUER & ARC from SELLA

Mount 'Endorphin'

Sella is a bit of a magnet for mountaineers, climbers coming from all over Europe to camp out in the woods, bed down at the **Font de l'Arc** refuge, and clamber all over the place, clinging to death defying precipices and swinging about in the void as only climbers can. The moment you arrive, you can appreciate why. Surrounded by dramatic cliffs that put the wind up me just to look at them, this is the sort of place to get the adrenalin rushing and the endorphins pumping, or whatever it is that possesses people to engage in such stunts.

For our part, we eschew the cliffs (though we get a good look at them) and opt for a more bucolic outing, following good paths and dirt tracks round the twin valleys of **Xarquer** and **Arc**, linking the two with the immaculately tailored route through the **Passet del Golero**.

3 | 3H 30M | 13 km | 400m / 400m | ↻ | 2

Access: Sella lies on the CV770 north of **Villajoyosa**. From the eastern end of the village, we take the lane to the northeast, signposted 'Cementeri', 'Barranc del Arc', 'Font de l'Alcantara' (there's also a mapboard for the **PRs 9 & 12**, which follow this road), bearing right at the rubbish bins and mapboard a couple of hundred metres later. When the tarmac ends a little over four kilometres from the CV770, we fork right and park 50 metres later in front of the **Font de l'Arc** refuge.

From the refuge car park (Wp.1 0M), we simply continue along the dirt track, following the **PR12**, which coincides with our itinerary for nearly four kilometres. The track climbs gently, first to the east then to the west, passing two minor branches off to the right at the first bend and numerous illicit camping bays tucked into the woods, the popularity of which are not one whit diminished by a profusion of signs prohibiting camping. This disdain for regulation is echoed at the first major Y-junction, where we fork right (Wp.2 22M): the private property sign on the left explicitly forbids climbing; glance over your shoulder at the rock face beyond the **Foia Roja** and there is every likelihood you'll see some blithe spirit dangling from the cliffs.

Thereafter, the **Tajo de Roldan** (the notch in **Puig Campana**) and the crests of **Els Castellets** come into view, and a superb panorama opens over the wild terrain surrounding the **Barranc del Xarquer**. Forking right at the next Y-junction (Wp.3 38M), we pass behind the **Maset del Secretari**, indicative of a charming phenomenon in the Costa Blanca mountains, where every functionary seems to have had their very own pad in the countryside - just in the immediate vicinity of **Puig Campana**, we can find homes dedicated to doctors, sacristans, rectors, chaplains, captains, nuns, even God (mind you, He's everywhere), and some minion who was merely The Official.

waypoint 5

The track then descends and levels out, bringing into view a small white cabin below the cliffs directly ahead of us. There are two clear indentations in the cliffs. The **Passet del Golero** is in the second, more northerly indentation. After passing the track accessing the white cabin (Wp.4 48M), we climb steadily, approaching a towering oblong monolith and a smaller, triangular pinnacle, where we leave the **PR12**. At the foot of the triangular rock the track we've been following so far levels out and veers right (signposted 'Finestrat') but we carry straight on (Wp.5 64M) along a track with a metal barrier against traffic (invariably raised), then turn left after ten metres on a narrow path marked by two stones, one with 'Benimantell' scratched on its face, the other daubed with a red arrow (Wp.6). At this point the present itinerary intersects with Walk 11, the route of which is the same for a little over three kilometres.

stone marker at Waypoint 6

Climbing briefly, we pass in front of a derelict *caseta*, after which we can see ahead of us the path that zigzags up to **Passet del Golero**. We dip down behind a dry reservoir then traverse a narrow terrace, beyond which a rough path, confirmed by a couple of cairns, descends to a Y-junction (Wp.7 72M). Forking right, we climb steeply to an intersection on the **Passet del Golero** (Wp.8 82M), where we turn right. 25 metres later, at a Y-junction where there's a rock with faded red paint indicating 'Finestrat' back the way we've come and 'Sella' to the left, we fork right for **Benimantell** (Wp.9). We now climb gently then steadily (NE) toward the obvious col separating us from the **Barranc del Arc**, following a narrow path hemmed in by holm oak, heather and pine, ignoring three forks down to the left (Wp.10 87M, Wp.11 & Wp.12), the first of which leads to the **Sirventa Living Art Gallery**, where tea and coffee are served if required.

Once on the col (Wp.13 102M), we can see the upper reaches of the **Barranc del Arc** and a clear track zigzagging up to the **Pas del Comptador** at its head. This track is the **PR9**, which

Passet del Golero

we follow back to the start, but which we join lower down in the valley. Descending from the col, we come to the end of another, narrower dirt track (Wp.14 108M), which we follow to the northeast, passing two cairn and waymarked paths branching off to the right (Wp.15 117M and Wp.16 120M), at the second of which, the present itinerary and Walk 11 diverge. We ignore both branch paths and stay on the track, which runs into a bend of another track a few metres later (Wp.17).

From hereon in, the route is very straightforward as we simply bear right, follow this track all the way to the intersection with the **PR9**, then take that back to the start, ignoring all branches en route. Descending into the basin of the rather unbarranco-like **Barranc del Arc**, we pass, in quick succession, one branch down to the left (Wp.18 126M) (a steep shortcut if you feel so inclined) and two to the right (Wp.19 127M and Wp.20 129M). Our track swings sharp right at a junction with another minor track coming in from the left (Wp.21 135M), after which we pass a house and descend through a lovely tapestry of pine, heather, holm oak, broom and rosemary, heading toward the **Isidor** caves below **Penyo Mulero**. At length, we join the **PR9** track at the point where it starts to climb steeply toward the **Pas del Comptador** (Wp.22 146M). Ignoring a minor branch descending to the left immediately after the junction, we carry straight on, and continue ignoring all branches, including a major track doubling back to the left (Wp.23 166M), three kilometres after which we arrive back at the **Font de l'Arc** refuge.

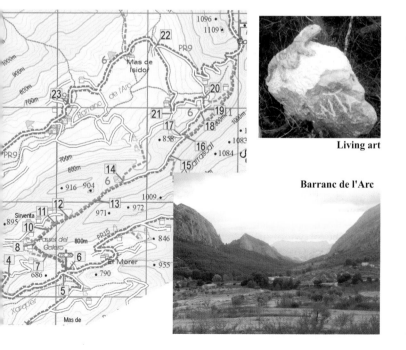

Living art

Barranc de l'Arc

Castell de Confrides

You know the castle at **Guadalest**, the one that appears on all the postcards and which is responsible for reducing the village to a parking lot with souvenir shops attached? Forget about it. This is the castle you want to visit.

Though barely better than a pimped up stroll, this is an extraordinarily gratifying little walk, featuring within a single square kilometre a bit of virtually everything you can expect to enjoy in the Costa Blanca mountains: scree, scrub, a scramble, crags, cliffs, vistas, a vertiginous eyrie, a pine wood, almond groves, terraces, a cherry orchard, and a castle perched on a pinnacle so improbably remote that you have to ask yourself just what they thought they were defending or, why they were so very, very scared. The short answer to that last question is - Christians.

The castle's original name was 'Alfofra' after the Moorish village it protected until 1264, when it was invested by Jaume el Conqueridor, King of Aragon and Count of Barcelona, architect of the shortlived Catalan empire, and a man who, for all his prodigious learning and patronage of the arts, was sufficiently bellicose to send anybody scurrying for the hills.

As with most despoiled strongholds, the history is dispiriting, but the site is magical. Particularly lovely as the sun sets and the rocks are gilded by the golden evening light until it seems the honey-coloured lustre is a property of the stone itself rather than an embellishment borrowed from the sun's rays. Bizarrely, access to the castle is not signposted and it is studiously ignored by the road hugging **PR44** that passes just below. If you don't do anything foolish, the top is not dangerous; however, it is vertiginous. The access road is a bit abraded and pot-holey in places, but never problematically so.

Access: Confrides is halfway between **Benidorm** and **Alcoi** on the CV70. From the sharp bend at km23.3 of the CV70, just east of the village, we take the asphalted track climbing to the south of the road, forking right 25 metres from the road, then left in front of the **Villa Font Freda** 500 metres later. Taking the right hand fork 900 metres after that, we climb on an increasingly narrow road (watch out for the overhanging pine!) for a further 900 metres until we reach a grassy parking bay on the right of the road just below the castle ideal for a picnic spot, too.

If this is occupied, there is plenty of roadside parking further along the road.

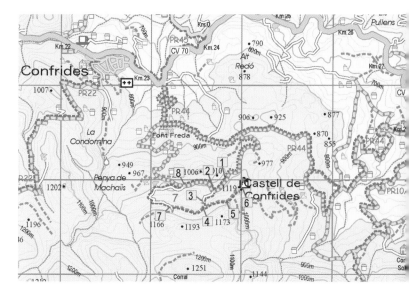

After the walk, we can continue to the west to return to **Villa Font Freda**, though the road taken on the way up is more attractive.

From the parking bay (Wp.1 0M), we simply stroll up the road for 200 metres, then fork left (Wp.2) on a dirt track. 10 metres before the end of the track, we fork left again on a stony path (Wp.3 6M) that climbs to the south before veering back toward the castle, passing a junction with another path coming in from the right (Wp.4 8M). At a small col overlooking **Benifato** and the **Partagat** track (Wp.5 12M), we bear left, following a clear but occasionally rough path that curves round the foot of the crags then climbs steeply to the outer fortifications and the remaining wall of the keep (Wp.6 22M), whereupon we all burst into a chorus of 'I'm the king of the castle'; infantile, I know, but it's that sort of thrill.

We return via the same route, save that at Wp.4, to extend the basic stroll and enjoy a less skittery descent, we fork left, continuing along a contour line before climbing very briefly to join a dirt track (Wp.7 45M). Bearing right, we follow the track as it meanders down through almond groves, passing a ruined cabin, from where we have perhaps the best view of the castle yet., before rejoining the road (Wp.8 57M). All that remains is to turn right to return to the start. Oh, yes, and there's that cherry orchard I promised you - on our left as we stroll back to the car.

8 CUMBRE DE AITANA from FONT DE L'ABRE (CONFRIDES)

This is the classic ascent of **Aitana**, the province's highest summit - or almost the classic ascent, but given a twist that turns it into a circuit. As with all the **Aitana** routes, the star of the show is the **Pas de la Rabosa**, an extraordinary little portal (I use the word advisedly; you half suspect you're moving into another dimension) through the rock that has to be seen to be believed. The climb to the top is brief but tough and there's a rough, pathless rockslide to be traversed on the descent which won't be to everybody's taste (any rougher and it ought to be subject to an Anti-Social Behaviour Order), specially since there's plentiful evidence of fresh spills. At the cost of sacrificing much of the adventure, the short version is a pleasant stroll avoiding all steep climbs and potential hazards, enjoying fine views that stretch to Ibiza on a clear day.

The only major issue is access. The traditional route to the **Font de l'Arbre** *area recreativa*, where our itinerary starts, was via a dirt track from **Port de Tudons** at the western end of the range. This is no longer recommended. It's still more or less drivable, but there are one or two deep puddle holes to be negotiated. The other approach, which is entirely asphalted and considerably more dramatic, involves some tricky steering at the start. The eastern access to **Confrides**, which is the most convenient to take for the turning in front of the bank (see below), is officially only an exit from the village, so you either have to ignore the 'no turning' signs or come in from the west, whereupon another dilemma presents itself. When the streets narrow in the centre of the village, the road we need doubles back to the right. This can be achieved in a small car with a very tight turning circle, a lot of shunting back and forth in a larger vehicle, or (what we always do and what the locals seems to do) driving through the village until just above the eastern exit, then turning round and driving all the way back (hoping nobody is coming the other way!) for an easy left fork.

*The **Alberg** at the start of the walk (closed Mondays) is so handy and so remote that it's worth recommending for location alone.

Access: Confrides is halfway between **Benidorm** and **Alcoi** on the CV70. From the eastern end of **Confrides** where there's a mapboard for the **PRs 20, 21 & 22**, we take **Carrer San Antoni**, the narrow lane climbing into the village from the CV70. 200 metres later, in front of the Caixa Callosa bank, we fork left on a narrow street signposted 'Font de l'Arbre 7km'. 100 metres after that we fork right, as indicated by a fingerpost for the **PR22** to 'Puerto de Tudons', a walking itinerary that corresponds with our drive to the **Font de l'Arbre** *area recreativa*. Following a good, surfaced track we climb steeply out of the village. Thereafter, there are places where the asphalt is a bit patchy, but it's consistent enough to qualify as a lane rather than a simple track, albeit in places a mildly alarming lane. We park in the large parking bays on the far side of the **Font de l'Arbre** *area recreativa*, 7km from the mapboard.

From the **Font de l'Arbre** *area recreativa* (Wp.1 0M), we walk back along

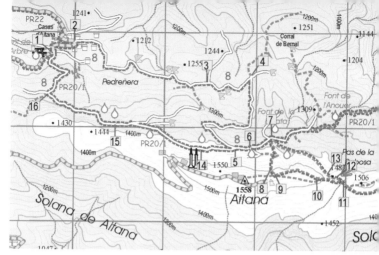

Wp.1

the **Confrides** road (N) for 350 metres, until the first sharp left-hand bend, where we turn right on a dirt track with a chain across the entrance and an 'Ayuntament de Confrides' sign prohibiting unauthorized vehicles (Wp.2). And that's pretty much all you need to know for now, as we simply follow this track until it joins the official route of the PR20 nearly 4½ kilometres later.

After a little under a kilometre on the track, we pass a small ruin and catch our first glimpse of the *forata*, an eye in the rock that lends its name to pretty much everything within shouting distance (snowpits, pinnacles, springs, they're all perforated round here), and which is just west of our descent via **Pas de la Rabosa**. After passing a second ruin, we skirt a pine wood, where we ignore a minor branch off to the left (Wp.3 28M 2.2km), sticking to the main track as it dips past a third ruin, at which point, if you look up to the right you'll see the military installations stretched along the back of **Aitana**. Our itinerary climbs onto the *cumbre* just to the left of the easternmost antenna. 50 metres after the ruin, we enter a second pine wood, where we ignore another minor branch off to the left (Wp.4 37M 2.8km) and swing sharp right, still following the main track as it climbs steadily to join the track used by the **PR20** (Wp.5 58M 4.4km)

Our return route is to the right, but for the present, we turn left, forking left 100 metres later (Wp.6 60M), and descend slightly to the **Font de Forata**, where we briefly intersect with Walk 9 (Wp.7 64M 5km). On the left at the head of the spring, the signposted 'Sender Botanic de la Paset de la Rabosa' branches off to the south-east. This is the route by which we descend. To reach the ridge though, we carry straight on, due south, in line with the troughs below the font, climbing directly towards the antennae and the military compound.

Font de la Forata

Following a clear path, we pass a PR cross a few metres later, then climb along the edge of a small hanger of pine. The path climbs steadily then steeply along the fringes of the wood, above which we can see the maintenance platform on the easternmost antenna we identified earlier. At the uppermost tree in the hanger (Wp.8 78M 5.5km), we bear left, following a faint trodden way climbing steeply across scree, eventually emerging 25 metres to the left of the easternmost antenna (Wp.9 88M 5.6km). Be prepared. If your breath hasn't already been taken by the climb (it probably has), it will be now by the views.

Bearing left, we follow a faint trodden way weaving over the rocks, picked out with intermittent PR waymarks. The path passes just below the cairn-capped rise of the highest point accessible to the public (the actual summit is in the military compound) before descending toward a shallow depression, where we will intersect with Walk 9 again. At a junction with another path that traverses the hillside lower down (Wp.10 97M 6.5km), we bear left to descend to the shallow depression. NOTE: If you approach the cliff's edge half way between Wps. 10 & 11, you can just pick out the **Pas de la Rabosa**, 100 metres to the north. When the path bottoms out (Wp.11 105M), we double back to the left towards a deep cleft, the far end of which appears to be blocked by a massive boulder of smooth rock.

.. squeeze down a second gateway ..

Rather than descending into the grassy gully preceding the cleft, we climb a faint stony trodden way (dotted with PR waymarks) along the right hand side of the cleft. The **Pas de la Rabosa** (invisible until the last moment) is immediately to the right of the smooth 'boulder', actually an outcrop of rock in its own right (Wp.12 109M 6.6km). We squeeze through the gateway, squeeze down a second gateway, then pick our way across two rockslides, the second old, the first alarmingly fresh. On the far side of the second rockslide, a rough path descends to join a clear path directly below the **Forata** (Wp.13 118M).

This clear path brings us back to the **Font de Forata** (129M 7.44km), from where it's all plain sailing, as we simply bear left and follow the PR track back to the beginning, passing the track we used on the outward leg, then (also on our right) two large snowpits (Wp.14 141M & Wp.15 153M), and enjoying the prospect of the spectacular cliffs below the **Aitana** ridge. Toward the end, we veer right to stay on the main track when a minor branch forks off to the left (Wp.16 163M).

Easier access, more paths than tracks, a wonderfully offbeat and little known way onto the uplands, an extended stretch on the crest, a constantly unfolding diorama of dramatic views, and, of course, the exhilarating escapade of **Pas de la Rabosa** (see Walk 8) make this splendid itinerary a serious contender for the preferred approach to the **Cumbre de Aitana**. The two walks are complimentary, but if you only have time for one, I'd recommend this route over Walk 8. A modicum of pathfinding confidence is required on the ridge due to the rough ground and patches of parallel paths. Otherwise, an easy (rockslide notwithstanding, again see Walk 8) and very gratifying little loop.

3 | 3H 10M | 10 km | 450m / 450m | ⟳ | 0

Access: Via **Benifato**, above the **Vall de Guadalest**, on the CV70 between **Benidorm** and **Alcoy**. From the CV70, we take the access road (S) toward the village. At the village limits sign, we turn right on a road marked with a ceramic plaque for 'Font de Partagat' and a 'PR21 Puerto de Tudons' fingerpost, setting the odometer at zero. After forking right at km1.8 and left at km2.4, we park in the *area recreativa* car park at the end of the road (km3.9).

From the end of the tarmac, we take the track climbing to the left of the 'Font de Partagas' (sic) sign (Wp.1 0M) for 'Sella PR10 17k', the **PR10** coinciding with our initial ascent. Ignoring a minor fork on the left after the first right-hand bend (Wp.2), we climb to a signposted Y-junction 50 metres later, where the **PR21** veers right for 'Puerto de Tudons' (our return route) and we fork left, staying on the **PR10** (Wp.3 6M).

our start at Wp.1

Climbing gently and enjoying some glorious views, we pass a path climbing to the right beside an information board about the local flora (Wp.4 13M) and a rough track descending to the left (Wp.5 21M). A little over 1500 metres from the start, the climb steepens as we approach the **Port de Tagarina**, just before which the track veers right, bringing into view a clear path snaking up the western slope above the port. This is the path we take onto the ridge, leaving both the dirt track and the PR.

Turning right at **Port de Tagarina** on a broad, stony trail (Wp.6 35M 2km), we embark on a steady to steep climb. 400 metres from the port, the path divides briefly (Wp.7 47M), the two branches merging again a few metres later, a pattern that is repeated several times during the climb. Thereafter, glorious views open out to the north again, rapidly complimented by a sweeping panorama to the south. The trail levels off before climbing again briefly to pass behind the first of three slope-shouldered rises above the cliffs on the northern side of the ridge (Wp.8 57M 3km). The first is unnamed, the second is the **Alt de Tagarina**, the third and largest the **Penya Alta**.

The walking is rougher here and there are intermittent stretches of parallel paths, but so long as you maintain a westerly direction and stay well back from the cliffs, the way is never in doubt. The only point at which the path is worth describing is on the eastern flank of **Penya Alta**. As you approach the **Penya**, you will see what appears to be a fissure in the rock giving the impression that half the mountain is about to split away and drop off. It ain't. In fact, the fissure is a rough groove in the rock. We bear left at the bottom of this groove to follow the clearer trodden way weaving (SW) through the scrub (Wp.9 72M), passing

The trail above Port de Tagarina

behind the oak-cloaked back of **Penya Alta**, from where we see the military and telecommunication installations on **Aitana** for the first time (Wp.10 77M 4km).

With these in sight, it's simply a question of keeping on keeping on, following the

clearer path until it dips into a shallow depression at the foot of the main mountain. This dip is riddled with sinkholes, some of spectacular dimensions, but the most important thing as we descend is to locate the **Pas de la Rabosa**. Off to the right you will see two deep clefts in the rock. The pas is immediately to the right of the larger cleft on the left. The cleft on the

Alt de Tagarina

right is a massive sinkhole of quite toe-curling dimensions.

Just short of the two clefts, we come to a junction of paths where the present itinerary intersects with Walk 8 (Wp.11 91M). If you don't intend doing Walk 8, turn left here and follow the PR waymarks up to the high ground outside the military installations, the actual summit of **Aitana** beng inside the green fence and coils of glistening razor wire (very valuable things, summits). To be honest, the views are not a lot better than those we've enjoyed so far, but they are more extensive, taking in the entire province and beyond Ibiza was visible the day we recorded this itinerary. If you do take this option, at the north-eastern corner of the military compound, where the narrow path used in the ascent of Walk 8 emerges (Wp.12 107M 5.5km), loop back to the left and contour across the mountainside on a faint trodden way back to Wp.11 (6.24km 120M). If you don't do this spur, cut 30 minutes and 1.4km from the total time and distance.

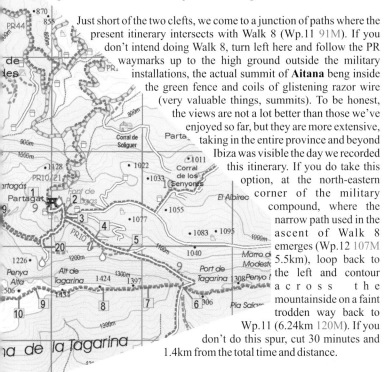

To reach the **Pas de la Rabosa** from Wp.11, we climb onto the right flank of the left cleft, where a faint stony trodden way (dotted with PR waymarks) approaches what appears to be a massive boulder of smooth rock blocking the way out. The **Pas de la Rabosa** (invisible until the last moment) is a gateway immediately to the right of the smooth 'boulder', actually an outcrop of rock in its own right (Wp.13 124M). We squeeze through the gateway, squeeze down a second gateway, then pick our way across two rockslides, the second old, the first alarmingly fresh. On the far side of the second rockslide, a rough path descends to join a clear path (Wp.14 133M 6.5km) directly below the **Forata**, a perforated rock visible from the second gateway.

This path brings us in easy stages down to the **Font de Forata**, below which we join a dirt track (Wp.15 145M 6.8km) and a signposted intersection of routes, at which point Walks 8 & 9 diverge. Turning right for 'Benifato', we ignore a fork up to the right 300 metres later (Wp.16) and a turning off to the left 180 metres after that (Wp.17 151M 7.3km). 225 metres later, the track dwindles to a path, 30 metres along which we ignore a fork off to the right (Wp.18 155M), staying on the main path as it descends to the **Font de l'Anouer**. A little over half a kilometre after the Font, the path comes to an intersection on a col immediately west of **Font de Partagat** (Wp.19 169M 8.5km), where we bear right, crossing the chaotic rubble of the **Runar de Partagat** to join a dirt track (Wp.20 177M 9.2km), on which we turn left to rejoin our outward route at Wp.4.

Good dirt tracks and broad trails, attractive countryside, a little visited ridge, and a perfect panorama make this itinerary ideal for smugly ticking off all the summits you've done at the end of a trip or, conversely, eagerly plotting the walks you plan to do in the coming days. The exertion rating is almost entirely for the brief but steep climb after **Port de l'Arc**, otherwise it's all easy strolling.

Access: To reach the start, we take the **Camino de la Sierra**, an asphalted track climbing to the west from km33.7 of the CV70 (east of **Benimantell**), where there is a large sign for 'Hostal El Trestellador', a small sign for 'Instituto RAM', and a large 'Generalitat Valenciana' panel concerning the track's upgrading consequent on flood damage. Ignoring a branch doubling back to the left after 200 metres, we continue along the *camino* for a further kilometre to the **Font del Moli Area Recreativa**, which is on our left. We park at the junction with the track accessing the *area recreativa*.

Font de Moli

Starting at Wp.1

From the entrance to the *area recreativa* (Wp.1 0M), we ignore the surfaced track leading to the font itself, which lies up to our right, and climb (SE) along a broad dirt track, passing between two *casetas*, one of which is helpfully called 'La Caseta'. The track climbs steadily, passing two major branches off to the left (Wp.2 and Wp.3 8M) and one to the right (Wp.4 13M), 50 metres after which, we fork left at a Y-junction (Wp.5 14M 1km).

Climbing amid healthy pine woods patched with terraces of olive and almond, we ignore a couple of minor branches accessing terraces, and simply enjoy the developing views, more of which anon when we reach the summit. After a long southeasterly trajectory, the track swings round to the right (SW), bringing into view the cliffs below **Penyo Mulero** and the delightfully named pinnacle of **Morro de Modesto** dwarfed by the cliffs behind it, it does indeed look like a very self-effacing lump of rock. Off to the right, on the next rise, we can just make out the crest path used in Walk 9.

Ignoring a grassy track forking off to the right (Wp.6 30M), we continue climbing above an attractive dell of cultivated land until we come to a broad,

below Wp.6

cairn-marked track forking left, the first major turning on the left since Wp.5 (Wp.7 36M 2.2km). Turning left then immediately forking right, we ignore a secondary fork on the right 50 metres later (Wp.8) and continue along a contour line running between terraces above the **Corral del Port** fields.

When the contour line runs into a terrace, we fork right on a much narrower track (Wp.9 41M 2.5km), again marked with a cairn. An easy, southeasterly climb brings us to the top terrace below a slope of scree, where another cairn marks our ongoing route, a narrow path traversing the scree (Wp.10 45M 2.8km). The path climbs gently to steadily across the scree, which is well settled and not at all loose underfoot, passing a small sinkhole, 60 metres after which we reach the rocky pass of **Port de l'Arc** (Wp.11 49M 3km), where the distinctive, notched silhouette of **Puig Campana** (Walk 3) comes into view.

The main cairn-marked route descends directly into **Barranc del Arc** (Walks 6 & 11) from here, but we turn right on a very narrow, but clearly visible path climbing along the ridge to the heights of **Penyo Mulero**. 300 metres later, we fork right at a Y-junction (Wp.12 54M), sticking with the clearer traces. The path divides very briefly a hundred metres further along (Wp.13), after which there is nowhere one might mis-doubt the way, and it's just a question of slogging up the slope. At the top of the slope, we join the end of a very rough dirt track (Wp.14 73M), 400 metres from the cairn-capped but otherwise undistinguished summit of the *penyo* (Wp.15 79M 4.2km), from where we can see more clearly the path used in Walk 9, snaking up the back of the next rise, and (off to our right) the rock on which **Castell de Confrides** is perched (Walk 7).

If you're new to the region, it's worth pausing between these last two waypoints to examine some of the other walking possibilities. We have already identified **Puig Campana** behind us. To the left of it, the shallow crab's claw silhouetted against the sea is **Monte Ponoig** (Walk 2). The jagged little ridge between the two defines the terrain circled in Walk 4.

El Castellet

To the north of **Ponoig**, we can see the hothouses of **Callosa d'en Sarria**, above which lies the jagged ridge of the **Serra de Bernia** (Walk 1). Directly north of us there's a fin-like rock of **El Castellet** which has been visible throughout most of the climb (Walk 17). To its right is the **Serra de Aixorta**, to its left **La Serrella**.

The easternmost summit on the **Serra de Aixorta** is the **Cerro de los Parados** (Walk 18). Immediately left of **El Castellet**, we can see the yellow scar of an overhang, which is at the foot of **Barranc de la Canal**, which we use in Walk 16.

Scanning west from there, the highest point, which looks very smooth and bland from this perspective (lot more interesting when you're actually on it), is the **Mallada del Llop** (Walks 15 & 16) and the next, equally bland looking rise (ditto), is **El Regall** (Walk 16). A little further west, we can see the discrete massif of **Pla de la Casa** (Walk 14). Beyond that, there is a long ridge patched with pine. The most westerly rise on the ridge, tonsured with a ring of pine, is **El Recingle Alt** (Walk 12). Directly behind **El Castellet** is the long hump of the Serra de Carrascal del Parcent (Walks 19 & 36).

From hereon in, it is all easy strolling. We continue along the track, soon descending to a major track at the **Port de Tagarina**, where we join the **PR10** and intersect with Walk 9 (Wp.16 89M 5km). Turning right, we follow the PR down toward **Font de Partagat**, a long, gentle descent blessed with glorious views, during which we pass two tracks doubling back to the right (Wp.17 100M and Wp.18 105M), and a signposted track (the **PR21**) doubling back to the left (Wp.19 111M). 50 metres after the intersection with the **PR21**, we leave the **PR10**, turning sharp right on a broad track traversing almond terraces (Wp.20).

Forking left 100 metres later (Wp.21 114M), we cross a stand of mature pine, immediately after which we ignore three branches off to the left, the first and last of which simply access terraces (Wp.22). At a Y-junction above a *caseta* and cherry orchard (Wp.23 126M), we fork left to descend past the orchard and the track accessing the caseta, after which there is no going wrong, as we simply stay on the main track, ignoring all branches, most of which merely access terraces. En route, we pass the ruined **Corral de los Senyores**, then descend through a spectacular gateway of rock, shortly after which we pass a snowpit (Wp.24 148M). 500 metres later, we rejoin our outward route at Wp.5, returning to the start via the same track.

11 BARRANCS DEL SALT, XARQUER & ARC

If looming crags, towering cliffs and spectacular rocks are your thing, look no further, this is the walk for you, a kind of 'Best of' sampling the highlights of the **PRs 9 & 15**, and linking them together with a loop round the climbing mecca of the **Barrancs del Xarquer** and **Arc** to create a sort of 'Now That's What I Call Rock' compilation. There's a three kilometre overlap with Walk 6, but the chances are you'll be fairly pleased to see somewhere comfortably familiar after the intimidating drama of the **Barranc del Salt**. I don't know its particular history, but the pass at the head of the **Barranc del Arc** is called the **Pas del Comptador**, a toponym customarily applied to a narrow gateway shepherds used for sheep-scoring. This example is not that narrow (see the alternative start to Walk 14 for a classic counting pass), but you can see how the bottleneck would have been useful with a large flock.

Access: To reach the start we take a surfaced track climbing to the south from the **Altet de Canonge** heights at km34.6 of the CV70 between **Benimantell** and **Polop**. If you're arriving from the west, the track is on the right. Immediately before the turning, there is a small white house on the left with 'Altet de Canonche' (sic) written on its face in large black letters. If you're coming from the east, the turning is on the left, 300 metres after the **Restaurants Vipas** and **Rincon de Pepe**. Ignoring all branch tracks accessing villas, terraces and *casetas*, we follow the surfaced track till the asphalt ends 700 metres from the road at the **Cuatro Vientos** villa, directly behind which there is room for three carefully parked cars. In the unlikely event that all spaces are taken, there is room for another car in the crux of the bend 200 metres along the dirt track.

waypoint 1

Torre de Dalt

From the **Cuatro Vientos** villa (Wp.1 0M), we continue along the same track, which is now unsurfaced, but still well-stabilized. Forking right after 240 metres (Wp.2), then turning left as indicated by cairns (Wp.3 4M), we leave the track and climb onto a broad balcony path, bringing into view the extraordinary cliffs that are the defining feature of this itinerary, and then, off to the left, the manicured grounds of the **Torre de Dalt** farmhouse.

the blade of rock seen from the east

At a crossroads of paths directly behind **Torre de Dalt** (Wp.4 13M), we carry straight on, the branch coming in from our right being our return route. The path is narrower here, but never in doubt, as we weave through the scrub below the cliffs, heading toward a spectacular blade of rock at the foot of the **Raco de les Tovaines**, which almost resembles a bracket bookending the mountain. 700 metres from the **Torre de Dalt** crossroads, we ignore a couple of cairns up to the right, and continue toward the blade of rock, shortly before which, the **PR15** feeds in from the left (Wp.5 22M 1.6km).

Carrying straight on again, we pass below the blade, which from this perspective better resembles a smooth sheet or sail, heading toward an apparent impasse. The path hugs the cliffs briefly, then veers away from a daunting rise to climb across a scrub clad shoulder striated with scars of rock. On the nearside of the shoulder, the path divides briefly (Wp.6 35M) and we fork right on the broader branch. Beyond the shoulder, we descend a little then follow a contour line overlooking the **Barranc de Gulabdar**, the approach used by the **PR15** from **Xirles**.

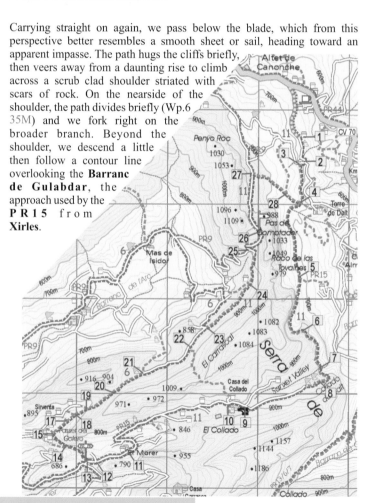

Barranc del Salt (Wp.7)

After descending again to a second cliff-hugging traverse below a looming overhang, we cross the upper reaches of the dry waterfall that lends its name to the **Barranc del Salt** (Wp.7 45M). Thereafter, a handful of zigs and a handful of zags bring us up the western flank of a far larger shoulder to reach the northern end of the **Sanxet** valley (Wp.8 53M).

Carrying straight on, we pass behind the principal **Sanxet** ruin, after which the path becomes an overgrown track, traversing terraces before climbing to a col. On the western side of the col, we join a clear dirt track beside a small helipad (Wp.9 65M), at which point we bear left toward a large, shuttered house. Just after the large house (Wp.10), there is a track doubling back on the right to a smaller house. Behind this house, there is a path crossing the ridge to Wp.22 in the **Barranc del Arc**. However, the way down from the top is a little obscure, so I recommend sticking to the track we're on, the **Cami de Sanxet**, for another two and a half kilometres before crossing into the next valley. This means descending an extra 150 metres and a corresponding climb, but it's all pleasant walking with fine views over the **Barranc del Xarquer**, and allows us to revisit the glorious **Passet del Golero** (see Walk 6).

After two kilometres, during which we ignore all branch tracks and paths, most of which are in any case chained off or sport private property notices, we pass the **El Morer** buddhist community (Wp.11 93M 6km). We continue descending steadily, ignoring a fork off to the right 400 metres later (Wp.12). 100 metres after that, we approach a major, signposted junction, where there's a metal barrier (usually raised) and the **PR15** intersects with the **PR12**.

Ten metres before the junction (Wp.13 100M), we turn right on a narrow path marked by two stones, one with 'Benimantell' scratched on its face, the other daubed with a red arrow. This is where we join Walk 6.

Climbing briefly, we pass in front of a derelict *caseta*, after which we can see ahead of us the path that zigzags up to **Passet del Golero**. We dip down behind a dry reservoir then traverse a narrow terrace, beyond which a rough path, confirmed by a couple of cairns, descends to a Y-junction (Wp.14 107M). Forking right, we climb steeply to an intersection on the **Passet del Golero** (Wp.15 115M), where we turn right. 25 metres later, at a Y-junction where there's a rock with faded red paint indicating 'Finestrat' back the way we've come and 'Sella' to the left, we fork right for 'Benimantell' (Wp.16).

We now climb gently then steadily (NE) toward the obvious col separating us from the **Barranc del Arc**, following a narrow path hemmed in by holm oak, heather and pine, ignoring three forks down to the left (Wp.17 120M, Wp.18 122M, Wp.19 126M), the first of which leads to the **Sirventa Living Art Gallery**, where tea and coffee are served if required.

Once on the col (Wp.20 134M), a fine vista opens out over the very domestic **Barranc del Arc**, at the far end of which we can see a clear dirt track snaking up to the **Pas del Comptador**, defined by two large pinnacles. This is the **PR9**, which we use briefly for our return.

Looking towards Pas del Comptador from Wp.20

Unfortunately, as is the tendency with cols, we now have to descend into the **Barranc del Arc**, where our path runs into the end of a rough dirt track (Wp.21 139M). 600 metres later, on the first rise, we pass a red-waymarked cairn marking the western end of the direct traverse from Wp.9 (Wp.22 147M). Our track then descends past a permanently inhabited house and, just before a sharp left hand bend, we fork right on a broad, recently cleared trail marked with a red arrow and a small cairn (Wp.23 152M), which follows a contour line and saves us from descending too far into the **Barranc del Arc**. This is where the present itinerary and Walk 6 diverge.

The trail approaches a small white house at the head of the valley, 100 metres short of which (Wp.24 161M), we fork right on a rougher path, again marked with small cairns and red waymarks. At first, it looks as if this branch is going to climb to the right of the more angular easterly pinnacle, but it almost immediately swings round to the left, joining the main PR track a couple of hundred metres below the **Pas del Comptador** (Wp.25 168M 10km). Turning right, we have a last steady haul up to the pass, where there is a **PR9** signpost (Wp.26 174M), at which point we return to the business of 'Now That's What I Call Rock'.

The track goes through a shady cutting, then winds along the foot of the cliffs below the **Penyo Roc**, fabulous views opening out over the **Vall de Guadalest** and toward the **Sierra de Aixorta**. 600 metres from the signpost on the pass (Wp.27 185M), we turn right on a narrow, cairn-marked path. Descending amid young pine, steeply at first then more gently, we pass an inverted Y-junction with a path coming in from the left (Wp.28 193M) 200 metres before rejoining our outward route at Wp.4 (196M 11.8km), where we turn left and follow the same route back to the beginning.

La Serrella is a glorious little range of mountains, a real walkers' playground; I must confess that, once I'd discovered it, I was hard pressed to drag myself away from the place, wanting to walk it every which ways I could, regardless of conditions, consequences, feasibility, and pretty much any other practical consideration you care to mention. This mildly deranged passion resulted in several walks so wild and woolly that they were completely unpublishable. Once you've seen these mountains, I hope you'll appreciate quite why I was slightly unhinged by their potential. Orology, topography, petrology, geomorphology . . . you can chuck around all the fancy words you like, **La Serrella** remains pure child's play in the truest sense of the term; to wit, absorbing, rewarding and indispensable.

The first of the itineraries we settled upon, following good (if not always drivable) dirt tracks all the way, is a fine outing taking us into the heart of the range with minimum effort, culminating at a small summit so perfectly placed that it's the site of a firewatch hut (you know you're onto something good when there's a firewatch hut up there), and giving us a glimpse of **La Serrella**'s most famous natural monument, **Els Frares** or 'the brothers', a congregation of rock needles and pinnacles that we visit closeup and considerably more precariously in Walk 13.

3 | 2H 30M | 11.5 km | 500m / 500m | 0

Access: The walk starts east of **Benasu**, which is towards the western end of the CV70 between **Benidorm** and **Alcoi**. Directly opposite the intersection of the CV70 with the CV770, we take the surfaced track to the north, passing signposts for the 'Cami de Quatretondeta' and 'Calvari', and a mapboard for the **PRs 23&24**, which coincide with two thirds of our itinerary. At the village **Calvary**, 100 metres from the main road, we turn right and follow a broad well-sealed track until the tarmac ends 1½ kilometres later. There's a layby on the left with room for two cars, otherwise there is ample parking at the bottom of the S-bend 300 metres earlier.

From the end of the tarmac, we carry on along its continuation as a stony track (Wp.1 0M), climbing to pass behind a fenced grove of olive and almond trees, 100 metres after which, we ignore a minor branch forking onto terraces on our right (Wp.2 7M).

Our start at Wp.1

Climbing steadily, occasionally steeply, we stick with the main track as it approaches a small pine wood on the flank of the mountain.

On the edge of the pine wood, the PR forks right, leaving the main track (Wp.3 24M), though there are no waymarks to indicate this and it scarcely matters, as the branch rejoins the main track 50 metres later. It's simpler to stay on the main track, bearing in mind that you might subsequently see waymarks on the parallel branch down to your right just before the two tracks merge.

Ignoring a branch off to the left at a major Y-junction (Wp.4 28M), we bear right, joining (100 metres later) the well-stabilized track that climbs from **Port de Confrides** on the CV70 (Wp.5).

Ahead of us we can see the peak of **Penya Alta**, which is where we leave the PRs. Bearing left, we follow this good track for a little over 1500 metres, until we come to a Y-junction on the **Coll de la Caseta del Rector** at the foot of the **Penya Alta**, where there is a large green firefighting reservoir (Wp.6 53M 3.5km).

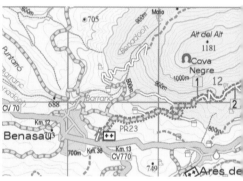

Turning left on the track behind the firefighting reservoir, we climb toward the ridge, doubling back to the northeast at a concreted bend, beyond which superb views open out towards the **Serra de Bernia**. The track levels out on the wooded tableland of **Pla de la Salvia**, where two branch tracks fork off to the right within ten metres of one another (Wp.7 64M), at which point we have two options, both desirable.

First, we take the second of the two branches on the right, and follow it across the pla until it ends 200 metres later (Wp.8 68M). Slightly to the right, an alley of pine trees defines a natural way passing a 'Microreserva de Flora' signpost. Staying to the right

at Wp.8

Fine views of 'the brothers (Els Frares)

of the signpost and picking our way over rocks and through gorse, cistus, and heather, we reach (some 75 metres from the end of the track) the top of a steep slope that functions as a natural *mirador* overlooking **Els Frares** (Wp.9).

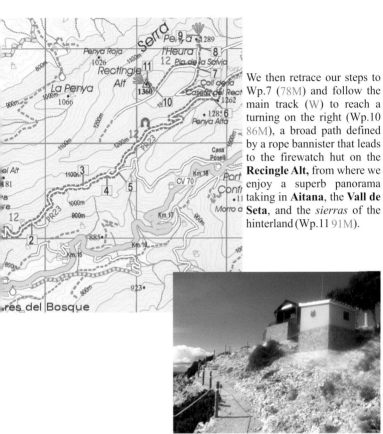

We then retrace our steps to Wp.7 (78M) and follow the main track (W) to reach a turning on the right (Wp.10 86M), a broad path defined by a rope bannister that leads to the firewatch hut on the **Recingle Alt,** from where we enjoy a superb panorama taking in **Aitana**, the **Vall de Seta**, and the *sierras* of the hinterland (Wp.11 91M).

The firewatch tower, Recingle Alt (Wp.11)

There is allegedly a route running the length of this ridge, which from this perspective looks rather appealing. However, the clear tracks and paths dwindle to nothing very discernible whatsoever at either end of the ridge. Having had a bash at both, I decided nobody would thank me for endeavouring to describe the indescribable and undesirable. We therefore return via the same route.

13 ELS FRARES

You'll find erosion sculpted pinnacles, finials, chimneys, columns, spires, stelae, towers, stacks, pillars and all manner of vertical rock formations throughout the Costa Blanca mountains, but nowhere is there quite such a remarkable and famous concentration as the **Frares** (the 'brothers' or 'friars') of **Quatretondeta**, an extravagant cluster of limestone needles that look spectacular from afar and are quite awe-inspiring once you get in amongst them. There, though, is the rub, 'getting in amongst them', because they are set amid precipitous slopes of scree laced with a maze of trodden ways, most of which go nowhere anyone sensible would want to go. Hence this rather curious double itinerary, the two ends of which are a mere 200 metres apart.

The Brothers

Our first exploration of this natural phenomenon, via the **Cami del Carrascal**, concluded with a little light rock-skiing and a scuffle with a collapsed pine wood that resembled a giant game of jackstraws before we eventually fetched up in somebody's back yard.

The second, via the **Cami des Clots**, on which I embarked with the GPS GoTo function switched on with a view to linking the two paths, was curtailed when I took the camera away from my face a bit too quickly and nearly fell off the side of the mountain with a sudden access of vertigo. Doubtless the two paths can be joined, but not by any route it would be responsible to publish in a book like this. If you only intend doing one of the options, the second is probably more spectacular, though a little more vertiginous. They are, however, complimentary, the first giving us a more comprehensive view of the ensemble. Bear in mind that, despite their brevity and relatively low exertion ratings, these are not easy walks. There is a real risk of vertigo and the terrain is very rough. Since we did not return by the same route, the overall time and (to avoid confusion) the distance for the first option are one way only.

A. via Cami del Carrascal

Access: Quatretondeta is between **Fageca** and **Gorga** on the CV754, which branches off the CV720 linking **Pedreguer** with the hinterland. We park on the main road into the village, the **Avinguda del Pais Valencia**, which is midway between km5 of the CV754 (if you're coming from the east) and **Font dels dos Xorros** (if you're coming from the west).

The walk starts opposite the junction of the **Avinguda** and the CV754, where the **Cami del Carrascal** (Wp.1 0M), at this stage a concrete track marked

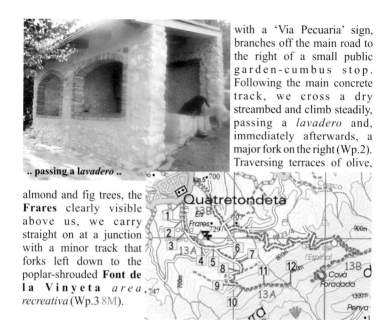

.. passing a *lavadero* ..

with a 'Via Pecuaria' sign, branches off the main road to the right of a small public garden-cum-bus stop. Following the main concrete track, we cross a dry streambed and climb steadily, passing a *lavadero* and, immediately afterwards, a major fork on the right (Wp.2). Traversing terraces of olive, almond and fig trees, the **Frares** clearly visible above us, we carry straight on at a junction with a minor track that forks left down to the poplar-shrouded **Font de la Vinyeta** *area recreativa* (Wp.3 8M).

After passing a tiny house on our left, we ignore one track forking right (Wp.4 13M) and two on the left (Wp.5 and Wp.6), after which the concrete ends (Wp.7 20M 1km).

The **Cami del Carrascal** continues as a stony dirt track, veering right 100 metres later, ten metres after which, we ignore a path climbing to the left marked by a boundary cairn (Wp.8). After climbing through a stand of mature pine and oak, the track crosses a couple of olive terraces and veers right once again, this time becoming far less well defined. At this point, we fork left on a minor branch marked with a cairn, heading toward the slopes of scree below the cliffs (Wp.9 30M 1.5km).

50 metres later, the branch track dwindles to a path beside a 'micro-reserva de flora' panel (Wp.10). Climbing steadily, we traverse a 100 metre stretch of scree, after which the path becomes more stable underfoot and fine views open out over the **Riu Seta** valley, which from this perspective has an almost Cappadocian aspect. Crossing a patch of cistus just before a large stand of oak, we pass a 'Generalitat de Valencia' metal post (Wp.11 41M). Beyond the oak, we traverse a second strip of scree, after which the climb steepens briefly before gradually levelling off.

Approaching the first of the 'brothers', we negotiate a third scree slope, this one partially composed of stones so large that it's almost a rockslide. On the far side of the main slide, directly below the most Rococo of the brothers, we reach a faint T-junction of 'ways' (I hesitate to call them paths) (Wp.12 51M 2.2km). From here it is 'possible' either to climb onto the **Serrella** ridge to join Walk 12 at Wp.7 or to descend to the **Cami des Clots** just below Wp.5 of option 2. Neither possibility is recommended though, so we return the same way.

B. via Cami des Clots

3 | 2H 25M | 6 km | ⛰ | ↗ 375m ↘ 375m | ⚠ | ⇄ | 🍴 3

Access: Immediately east of **Quatretondeta**, at km5 of the CV752, we take the **Cami des Clots** (aka **Cami de la Font Roja**), a surfaced track marked with a mapboard and fingerposts for the **PRs 23 & 24**, which we follow for the main climb. The concrete surfacing ends 200 metres from the road, after which the **Cami des Clots** becomes a good dirt track. 125 metres later, we park on the right, in a large layby with room for half a dozen cars.

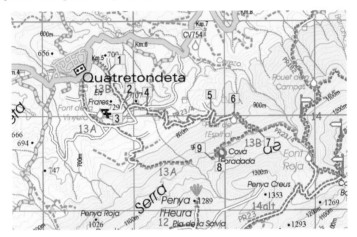

From the layby (Wp.1 0M), we simply follow the main track and its PR waymarkings all the way till it ends at the **Font del Espinal**, the **Frares** visible above us throughout. At the time of writing, the route is clearly waymarked and ought to remain so, but in case this is no longer the case, we carry straight on at the crossroads 150 metres from the layby (Wp.2) and fork left 50 metres after that at the **Carrasca de la Tia Sofia**, a large oak tree named after the land's former owner (Wp.3). Forking right at the next Y-junction (Wp.4 9M), we pass a tiny, two storey cabin, decked out with a diminutive balcony, after which the track becomes stonier and steeper. 150 metres after a second, larger cabin, we pass a very rough branch doubling back to the left (Wp.5 26M) and an information board describing the flora around the **Frares**.

Font de l'Espinal

The track ends at the **Font de l'Espinal** (Wp.6 33M 2km), behind which there is a gravity challenged almond tree propped up on a couple of makeshift crutches. Still following the PR (though it's not initially waymarked as such), we continue on a broad trail that soon dwindles to a path, climbing steeply through a hanger of pine, which is so badly beaten about by disease and storm damage that many of the old traverses are blocked by fallen trees, as a consequence of which, former shortcuts have become the official path. Above the wood, we pass three 'Sender Botanic de les Fonts' information boards, the third under a low cliff with a concave, water-streaked midriff (Wp.7 50M 2.4km). At this point, we leave the PR, which carries on climbing to **Font Roja** and **Pla de la Casa** (Walk 14), and turn right on a faint way trodden into the scree, heading directly toward the **Frares**. **NOTE:** Even at this stage, the easy part of the approach, care should be taken. Stop to admire the unfolding spectacle, but keep your eyes down while you're walking.

The 'way' briefly resolves itself into a proper dirt path 100 metres later as it veers towards the cliffs and a tiny cave, after which it becomes increasingly indistinct, the more so as the slopes get steeper. Just how far you continue here is going to be a question of taste, temerity, and curiosity. Most people will want to turn back after about 400 metres, when the 'path' such as it is, dips into a declivity and starts climbing steeply. The more foolhardy may care to follow me! Though please bear in mind that descending from Wp.9 back to the scree path is considerably more painstaking, time consuming, and all round alarming than ascending.

The tail end of the walk is only 100 metres or so, preceding a tall wall of rock with two distinct eyes drilled through its upper reaches, but it's sufficiently hair raising to s e e m   m u c h   l o n g e r . Approaching the wall, the trodden way climbs steeply along exposed dirt and grit, bringing the skylight arch of the **Cova Foradada** into view on our left, which can be reached by a very steep scramble (Wp.8 66M).

approaching waypoint 8

Actually getting into the cave itself requires climbing skills I'm not prepared to acquire, but if the folly doesn't seem too great (it probably is), it's possible to push on a little further to get right inside the cluster of needles behind the tall wall of rock. Hugging the cliffs directly after the *cova*, we pick up a way that is essentially pathless, whatever goats and local outward bound enthusiasts claim, climbing to a narrow and precipitous pass within the heart of the needles (Wp.9 74M 3.14km). Any further and you're on your own! We return via the same route.

The highest summit in **La Serrella** and the heart of this wonderfully wild landscape, **Pla de la Casa** would be a privileged spot even without the addition of a nigh on perfect PR. As it is, one would be hard pressed to think of another mountain in the region better served by the pathmakers. I say 'nigh on perfect' because the trail does have one basic fault, taking in too much tarmac in its last quarter, a flaw remedied here by the simple expedient of returning to the start via the **Cami del Comte Meiral** rather than the **Cami de l'Olivar**. The summit was the site of the highest Moorish castle in the region, but there's precious little to see of the fortifications nowadays, just the base of some walls. However, the plateau that lends its name to the mountain does boast a remarkable and remarkably well-preserved eighteenth century snowpit, the *Cava* or **Pou de Neu**, with a capacity of over a thousand cubic metres which is to say, if a moment of idle fancy is to be trusted (it's probably not), that you could get about twenty elephants in there, always supposing you were of a mind to do so and they were of a mind to comply.

The descent to **Coll de Borrell** is quite exposed, not enough to merit a vertigo warning, but enough to suggest that some might find it a bit 'airy'. The alternative approach from the south is merely that, an alternative for those who find it more convenient to climb from above the **Guadalest Valley**. It's an attractive route and the traverse below the **Cantalar de Gil** is quite splendid, but it is precipitous, particularly in descent, and won't be to everybody's taste.

| 4 | 3H 40M | 9.4 km | ⏶ 565m ⏷ 565m | ↻ | 🍴 0 |

Short Versions

(a) Cova de Bernat or **Font del Cuquero**

(b) Bear left at Wp.12 to pass to the right of the 'burial cairn' and follow the alternative approach in reverse (Wps.15-12) to **Coll de Borrell**, thus cutting out the summit and rejoining the main itinerary at Wp.16.

Access: The walk starts from **Fageca** (aka **Facheca**), which is between **Castell de Castells** and **Gorga**, at the western end of the CV720 linking **Pedreguer** with the hinterland.

The village church backs onto the CV720, 100 metres east of the intersection with the CV754 and immediately west of the **Casa Rural Masanet**. There is a bus shelter here and two tall pine trees, behind which there is a mapboard of the route. We park beside the two tall pine trees.

Directly behind the pine trees, just below the sign for 'Placa de l'Esglesia', we take a paved track on the right passing under the CV720 (Wp.1 0M).

Our start point (Wp.1)

Barranc del Moro

100 metres later, the paving gives way to concrete as we head southeast towards the **Barranc del Moro**, the scree-grizzled top of which is is clearly visible ahead of us. 250 metres from the village, the **PR168** veers left for 'Famorca' (Wp.2 4M) and we fork right on a dirt track climbing toward the ravine.

A steady climb brings us to a Y-junction, where we turn left (Wp.3 9M), as indicated by a cairn and a waymark, on a dirt track leading to a terrace of olive trees 100 metres later. Just before the terrace, we bear right on a broad trail (Wp.4) that dwindles to a rocky path as it curves into the lower reaches of the ravine, where it runs along a retaining wall above abandoned terraces. After crossing a watercourse three times in quick succession, we climb steadily, passing a shortcut marked with a PR cross (Wp.5 31M). A series of scree-laden shortcuts ensues as we continue to climb, bringing into view off to our right **La Cova de Bernat**.

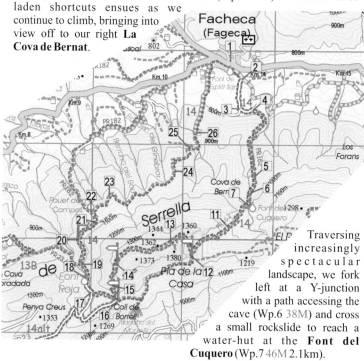

Traversing increasingly spectacular landscape, we fork left at a Y-junction with a path accessing the cave (Wp.6 38M) and cross a small rockslide to reach a water-hut at the **Font del Cuquero** (Wp.7 46M 2.1km).

Ignoring a profusion of goat paths off to the left, we bear right behind the waterhut, climbing alongside a line of large rocks. Ignoring three branches on the left (Wp.8 / Wp.9 / Wp.10) and one on the right (Wp.11 59M), we stick to the main path, climbing southwest. The gradient eases after Wp.11, from where we can see what looks like a large burial cairn (actually an outcrop of rock) directly ahead of us and, a little to the right of the 'cairn', a finger post.

The path to the top climbs across the scree to the right of this post (NNW). A steady climb, in the course of which the **Cumbre de Aitana** with its distinctive radar dome comes into view, brings us to the finger post, where we turn right, now climbing to the north (Wp.12 79M 3km), bringing into view a *finestra* off to our right. Climbing steadily to steeply on a stony path, we eventually cross a small rise and come to the superb snowpit situated directly below the **Pla de la Casa** summit (Wp.13 93M 3.45km). The ongoing path is a little obscure at first, but clear waymarks directly behind the snowpit indicate our way across the plateau, weaving through the scrub toward two pine and a small outcrop of rock. Passing directly behind the outcrop of rock and its satellite pinnacles, we recover a clear path traversing the western reaches of the *pla*, a glorious vista opening out to the north. At the southwestern end of the *pla*, we pass a waypost (Wp.14 104M) and begin our descent on a broad path weaving through clumps of broom toward the **Port de Confrides** dirt track used in Walk 12 and the alternative start.

PR signposts at Wp.18

About two thirds of the way down, we cross a lip of rock, below which we ignore a very faint branch off to the left (Wp.15 117M). After a final, skittery stretch, the path bottoms out on the **Coll de Borell** (Wp.16 123M) and we turn right for 'Fageca por Font Roja'. Following a narrow path meandering through a scattering of pine trees, we descend to join a branch of the **Port de Confrides** track (Wp.17 128M), where we turn right, bringing into view a diminutive, triple *finestra*. 100 metres later, the dirt track ends at the **Font Roja**, where the **PRs 23&24** fork left, and we turn right to cross the **Barranc Fondo**, still following the **PR182** (Wp.18 133M 5.15km).

Dipping into the **Barranc Fondo** watercourse, we immediately climb onto the ravine's eastern flank to follow a faintly alarming looking path, a goat track readily distinguishable from the far bank as a white stripe running across the hillside. In fact, it's wider than it looks, but you still need to be fairly sure-footed this is a goats' path after all! For the first 150 metres, the path climbs gently, then levels out to follow a contour line leading to a small rise and into a 250 metre stretch of scree (Wp.19 142M).

Having traversed the scree, we cross a rocky spur where there is a waypost (Wp.20 149M) and the path swings round to the right (NE), still following a contour line as it approaches a stand of pine. We pass above the pine, the path becoming a little less goat-like and a bit more ramblerish, though it's still largely defined by scree. At a faint Y-junction (Wp.21 156M), we fork left, as indicated by cairns and waymarks, descending on a narrow path, initially trodden into loose scree then on a base of red dirt, heading toward the village of **Benimassot** on the far side of the **Vall de Seta**. A little over 100 metres later, we reach the **Pouet d'en Campos** well, where there is an old stone drinking trough (Wp.22 164M), at which point we leave the PR. The official route of the PR carries straight on here, but to reduce the road walking, we turn right on a good path, bringing **Fageca** into view shortly before we pass a solitary pine (Wp.23 169M). The path curves round the head of three gullies, the first (**Barranc del Bou**) including a long stretch on scree, the second (nameless) striated with ancient terraces, and the third (**Barranc del Ginebrar**) preceding our final descent. On the far shoulder of **Barranc del Ginebrar** (Wp.24 186M), we bear left, following a winding way weaving between pine trees and traversing abandoned terracing, descending toward the end of a lane, the **Cami del Comte Meiral**. A little way above the lane, at a T-junction with a terrace path (Wp.25 197M), we turn right, following the clearer traces down to reach the end of the lane (Wp.26 203M 8.3km), 1500 metres from the village.

.. an old stone trough (Wp.22)

Alternative approach to Pla de la Casa from the south

4 | 1H 30M | 4.1 km | 335m / 335m | ⚠ | ↔ 0

Access: The alternative approach to **Pla de La Casa** starts between **Confrides** and **Port de Confrides** on a broad dirt track branching north at km19.4 of the CV70. We park in the spacious bend at the bottom of the track. Before setting off, it's worth stepping back and looking up at the rocks directly behind the dirt track, where there is a long line of craggy pinnacles, to the left of which there is a larger monolith, and to the left of that a long stretch of pine. The **Pas del Comptador** is between the monolith and the craggy pinnacles. The route is roughly waymarked with unofficial PR-style waymarks.

Wp.1 - our start point

From the road (Wp.1 0M), we walk up the track to a triple junction (Wp.2 6M), where we fork left, climbing towards **Les Bardals**, the craggy pinnacles noted earlier. After passing a fork accessing a *caseta* on the right (Wp.3 10M), we see a large rock window, the **Recingle Finestra**, off to our right.

The track gets rougher the higher we climb and eventually peters out altogether beside a large cairn and an arrow composed of stones (Wp.4 18M) indicating a rough way doubling back to the left above the track. The way, which rarely aspires to pathdom, climbs steadily then steeply, picked out by cairns and the occasional waymark, weaving through sparse scrub between the pine wood on our right and the **Barranc del Pinar** on our left. Passing to the right of a first long outcrop of rock (Wp.5 29M), we continue climbing steeply, more or less straight up insofar as the terrain allows, to a second outcrop of rock (Wp.6 32M). Above the second outcrop of rock, the path, now

The arrow of stone (Wp.4)

identifiable as such, veers left, following a contour line along an ever so slightly vertiginous stretch above the ravine, before a final, brief climb across bare rock brings us to the pass (Wp.7 43M). At this point, the waymarked route hugs the rocks off to the right to reach Wp.10, but for a slightly clearer, cairn-marked route we descend towards **Font de Serra**, the trough of which is clearly visible off to the left. After a brief, easy, off-path descent on bare rock and scree, we cross a runoff channel and skirt a small field to reach the Font (Wp.8 48M), from where a rough path climbs to join the tail end of a very rough dirt track cum firebreak (Wp.9 51M). Turning right on the faint remains

of an older track, we pass directly behind the walls of an ancient ruin 75 metres later, after which a clearer track climbs to join the principal, well-stabilized track from **Port de Confrides**, which coincides with the **PR23**, a section of which is used in Walk 12 (Wp.10 56M). Carrying straight on along the PR, we approach the scree-flanked rise of **Pla de La Casa**. The track descends to a junction (Wp.11 64M 2.4km), at which point we veer right (leaving the **PR23**) to reach **Coll de Borrell**, where the track ends at a signposted intersection with the **PR182** (Wp.12 70M) (Wp.16 of 14 main).

From here, we take the un-signposted path to the right, maintaining an easterly direction to reach a junction with another path on the right (Wp.13 76M) that leads to an attractive natural *mirador* overlooking the **Barranc del Monesillo**. After enjoying the views, we return to the main path to traverse the scree laden slopes below the impressive pinnacles of the **Cantalar del Gil**, heading towards a clump of holm oak on a spur on the horizon.

About halfway across the base of **Pla de la Casa**, the path has been swallowed up by a rockslide above an absolutely ginormous 'boulder', into which a little shelter has been built (Wp.14 86M). Bearing slightly left, we continue to climb along the edge of the scree above the boulder shelter, our route confirmed by a couple of cairns, and soon reach a clear path passing in front of the clump of holm oak we saw earlier, after which we come to a crossroads of paths (Wp.15 92M). 50 metres to the left, is the fingerpost at Wp.12 of the main walk, which we follow through waypoints 12 to 16 back to **Coll de Borrell**.

The **Mallada del Llop** is one of those summits that beguile not because of what they are, but because of what's around them. No soaring peaks or jagged crags here. Just a humpy bit, barely distinguishable from the other humpy bits around it and, not to put too fine a point on it, covered in sheep shit. But the views are stupendous, the **Clot del Noguer** lovely, the **Barranc de la Canal** a superb piece of natural engineering, the sense of being somewhere high and wild and wonderful almost overpowering, and the path for the main climb so beautifully graded that one barely notices one's climbing at all. Not so little then? Read the Big Wolf (Walk 16) and you'll understand the title. **Mallada del Llop** means Sheepfold of the Wolf, which sounds a bit self-defeating in English, but doubtless has a better ring to it in Catalan, and presumably refers to a point of refuge or corral in the days when wolves roamed these mountains. The wolves are long gone, but you'll see plenty of sheep and goats, and possibly a sounder of wild boar, too, the latter having cannily cottoned onto the fact that these heights may not offer much in the way of cover, but are pretty handy since this area is a reserve where hunting is prohibited.

This is the classic ascent, so very classic that it ought to be a PR, an oversight one can only suppose a consequence of the pathless business on the top. Well, it's not so much pathless. There are thousands of the things. Endless goat tracks, none of them going anywhere, encasing the mountain in a baffling web of "What's over there", "I'm going this way, me", and "I wonder what would happen if?". Try to follow a clear path for the last 100 metres of the climb and you'll rapidly be reduced to a gibbering wreck. Accept the inevitable and follow your nose (or your GPS) and you'll have a ball. For this reason, clear conditions and a certain amount of route finding confidence are required for the full walk. The short version is suitable for all and highly recommended of itself.

Short Version: the **Clot del Noguer** is a lovely spot for a picnic.

Access: Our itinerary begins in **Famorca**, which lies to the west of **Castell de Castells** on the CV720 linking **Pedreguer** with the hinterland. From the eastern side of the village, take the Centre Urba access road then park on the right 100 metres later, alongside the village's diminutive sports ground, 50 metres from the *lavadero* in **Plaza La Font**.

The walk starts between the parking area and the *lavadero*, opposite a small public garden, immediately after three recycling bins and a mapboard for the **PR168**, which runs into **Famorca** on a concrete track doubling back to our left. Ignoring a PR cross, we set off on a second concrete

start point at Wp.1

track, the **Cami de la Rabosa**, that forks off to the left just beyond the mapboard (Wp.1 0M).

Climbing along the **Cami de la Rabosa** to the south, we soon see a couple of the white water inspection huts along the line of the interred canalization pipe which brings the village's drinking water down from the **Font del Noguer**, the course of which is shadowed by our initial ascent.

As the **Cami de la Rabosa** swings left to cross a watercourse, we ignore a rough track climbing to the right, and turn right 10 metres later, immediately after the watercourse, on a narrow, stony path shored up with a rough, drystone retaining wall (Wp.2 7M).

our narrow, stony path at Wp.2

Although unmarked, once you're on it, the path is unmistakable and the book can be safely stowed until we reach the mini-cirque of **Clot del Noguer**. Climbing alongside the deepening gully of the watercourse, our path briefly touches on a bend in a branch of the **Cami de la Rabosa**, which we ignore, veering right (Wp.3 15M) to continue on the path, re-crossing the watercourse 100 metres later. And that's all you really need to know for now. The path continues to climb steadily through beautifully graded traverses, passing three very minor maintenance paths forking right to reach inspection huts (Wp.4, Wp.5 and Wp.6 40M) and two inspection huts themselves.

There are a couple of obvious and obviously redundant shortcuts, but when we draw abreast of a third hut, we come to a more distinct Y-junction, where it's worth noting that we ignore the shortcut that carries straight on and instead bear left to follow the main path (Wp.7 58M). 100 metres later, we pass a shepherd's shelter under an overhanging rock and emerge in the idyllic little

Clot de Noguer

cirque of **Clot del Noguer**, where a stand of poplar and a patch of damp ground announce the imminence of the spring.

Still following a clear path, we cross the **Clot** (SE) to reach the **Font del Noguer** (Wp.8 64M 2.3km).

Ignoring paths to left and right, we carry straight on (S) directly behind the spring to reach a snowpit, visible from the font, where we turn left (Wp.9 68M) on a narrow but clear path climbing toward a small, partially walled cave, to the right of which there's a tiny finestra. Halfway between the snowpit and the cave, the path divides (Wp.10). Either branch will do. The left fork passes below the cave then veers right to climb a faint way trodden in the scree of a shallow gully, the right fork passes above the cave before climbing along the flank of the gully. Either way, once past the cave we can see the distinct V of a col, which we cross a little way to the right of the V's base, at which point we can see the sea and, immediately ahead, a second col, separated from the first by a shallow depression (Wp.11 86M 2.9km).

The paths have been sketchy for the last few hundred metres, but you can forget about them altogether now or they'll drive you barmy. Immediately to our right, two cairns indicate the beginnings (only the beginnings, mind) of a reasonably clear 'way' heading southwest. The clear way peters out a couple of hundred metres later (Wp.12), but maintaining a southwesterly direction amid the sparse vegetation and contouring round a shallow gully behind the snowpit and font, we soon come onto the ridge, from where we see the **Sierra de Aitana** (Wp.13). From here, we simply turn left and follow the ridge up to the trig point on the summit, which is only visible towards the end (Wp.14 101M).

100metres to the NE of the trigpoint, there is another small rise topped with a cairn (Wp.15). Just below this rise, a reasonably clear goat track heads west. After 300metres, slightly to the left of the ridge, we come to a signless, rusted metal signpost (Wp.16 108M). Directly below, we can see the clear path traversing the second col and descending into the **Barranc de la Canal**. Once again, we put aside any pretence at following an identifiable path and pick our way down the slope toward the clear path, taking care on the loose stones and tracing out sufficient traverses to break the gradient. Once back on the clear path (Wp.17 115M), we simply turn left to return to the first col and Wp.11 (120M), then follow the same route back to **Famorca**.

If there's one slight drawback to Walk 15, it's that we labour all the way up to the top and then we labour right back down again. For most summits, doing a 'Grand Old Duke of York' is unavoidable, but in this respect, the very indistinctness of **Mallada del Llop** is its strength, for it is part of a long line of rock that just begs to be walked in its entirety, which is why we were tempted to go back again. We didn't regret it, either. In fact, it was one of our most memorable days out during the course of our researches.

the ridge between the two summits

This is wonderful wild walking in awe-inspiring terrain, much of it off path with corresponding rewards. For those who love getting off the beaten track, it's an absolute must, especially the spectacular ridge walk between **Mallada del Llop** and **El Regall** (aka **Pic de Serrella**).

For the most part, the offpath stretches are easy, however, I recommend doing Walk 15 first to get the lay of the land. It's also useful to have done Walk 17 before in order to have an overview of the fabulous little **Barranc de la Canal**, though one should bear in mind that the *couloir* is not nearly so steeply raked as it appears from the east. It's also worth mentioning that, from Walk 17, the path between Wps.11 and 12 is undetectable. You have to be on it to see it. There is a very slight risk of vertigo in the traverse preceding Wp.10.

Access and the start are the same as for Walk 15.

4 | 4H 15M | 10.3 km | 660m / 660m | ⚠ | ↻ | 🍴 3

As per Walk 15, we set off on the **Cami de la Rabosa** from **Famorca** (Wp.1 0M), except this time, when the track crosses the watercourse after 325 metres (Wp.2 4M), we ignore the path up to the right and continue on the *cami*, passing two concrete tracks branching off to the right (Wp.3 and Wp.4). 150 metres after the second concrete branch, the **Cami de la Rabosa** dwindles to a broad trail (Wp.5 13M) that soon shrinks to a narrow path beside a roughly daubed PR style waymark (Wp.6 16M 1km). Though faint, these unofficial waymarks (this isn't actually a PR) are occasionally useful, particularly at the lower end of **Barranc de la Canal**.

The path climbs across abandoned terraces below the aptly named crags of the **Aspres de Famorca** (*aspres* is cognate with asperity and means 'rough, surly, sour, harsh, gruff"), disappearing occasionally in sheets of rock, but so long as we maintain a southeasterly direction (aiming for the small conical rise to the left of the **Aspres**) and keep climbing, the clearer traces soon reveal themselves. After a few hundred metres, we zigzag up a spur on a better defined path, then contour round the heads of three gullies (Wp.7, Wp.8 and

Wp.9 55M). **NOTE:** In the third gully, the path is narrow and runs along the edge of a crumbling terrace wall, so some care is required about where you put your feet.

On the eastern edge of the third gully, we pass a much brighter waymark, from where we can see the distinctive pinnacles of **El Castellet** (Walk 17) and **Cerro de los Parados** (Walk 18) (Wp.10 58M). Also visible are the folds of two more gullies and, beyond them, a small hanger of pine silhouetted against the horizon, which is where we will bear south toward **Barranc de la Canal**. The path here is largely maintained by sheep and goats and suffers the usual problem with such routes, to wit, all manner of capriciously engineered splinter trails running parallel to one another. Nonetheless, the main path remains clearer than the others and is relatively easy to follow.

After crossing a small rise, we dip down to pass directly behind the hanger of pine (Wp.11 75M 3.3km), beyond which a reasonably maintained terrace path bears south, bringing into view a tiny col at the tail end of the **Aspres**, pricked by the silhouette of a municipal boundary sign. This is where we cross into the *barranc*. The path becomes obscure again as we approach the col, but directly below the sign we come to a T-junction with a clear path (Wp.12 85M).

The branch to the left joins Walk 17, but we turn right, as indicated by another faint PR style waymark and a yellow arrow, and descend along a rough, but sufficiently clear, cairn-marked way into the scorched lower reaches of **Barranc de la Canal**, where cairns and waymarks (Wp.13 96M) indicate a way across a rockslide to pick up the intermittently clear path we follow to the top of the *barranc*.

Barranc de la Canal

There are three snowpits in the ravine, but they are discreet to the point of invisibility in this direction of travel, so it's best to concentrate on following the cairns and enjoying the wild terrain, as we are walled in by impressive crags, and accompanied by the usual bleating procedure that goats and sheep the world over seem to regard as an appropriate response to the approach of strangers.

At the top of the *barranc*, we come to a col between the **Aspres de Famorca** and the **Mallada del Llop**, within sight of a second col some 500 metres away. Immediately after passing a small cairn, we fork left on a faint trodden way (Wp.14 147M), which is where the off path stuff begins. There is no right way to do this. We followed a different route from the descent in Walk 15. It's just a matter of picking your way through the sparse scrub, following any one and very probably many of the myriad interlacing goat tracks, maintaining a westerly direction insofar as the terrain allows, and climbing steadily, though never steeply, aiming for the rocks up to the left above the second col.

We pass just to the right of the upper outcrop of rock to reach the **Mallada del Llop** trig point (invisible until the last moment) 100 metres later (Wp.15 163M 5.5km).

To the west, we can see the **Recingle Alt** ridge (Walk 12) and **Pla de la Casa** (Walk 14), on the nearside of which is our next objective, the slope-backed, cliff-faced summit of **El Regall**. Immediately to the north of **El Regall**, we can also see the clear path by which we descend to the **Clot del Noguer**.

climbing 'off path'

First, though, we have the unmitigated pleasure of a bit of 'top of the world' ridge walking. Heading west, we continue off path, enjoying easy walking amid the scattered clumps of hedgehog broom, while a splendid panorama unfolds around us.

After a few hundred metres, a fairly clear way resolves itself along the ridge, enough to be identified as a path, which continues, all appearances to the contrary from afar, to within 100 metres of the peak. An easy stroll across sparse grass and bare rock brings us onto **El Regall**, which is crowned with a summit cairn (Wp.16 187M).

descending into Clot del Noguer

Still off path, we turn right here and descend (NNW) past a solitary and seriously challenged pine tree to the obvious pass between the **Clot del Noguer** and **Barranc del Moro** (see Walk 14), where we come to two narrow, but clear paths running parallel with one another (Wp.17 193M). Turning right on the second of the two paths, we descend toward the **Clot del Noguer**, bringing into view the snowpit at its southern limit. The path gets rougher after a couple of hundred metres, but soon coalesces into a good dirt and grit path.

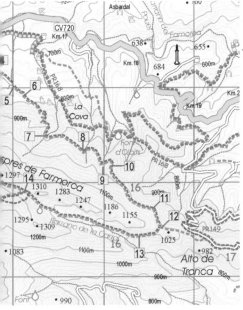

Almost in the middle of the **Clot**, we come to a distinct Y-junction (Wp.18 205M), where we fork left to reach the **Font del Noguer** (Wp.19 208M 7.9km).

If, as suggested, you did Walk 15 first, you'll know precisely where you are and what you've got to do next. If not, in brief, turn left at the *font* and follow the clear path round by the stand of poplar to the north, beyond which you'll find a small, walled overhang corral (Wp.20 212M), where the traditional ascent arrives.

Beyond here, you really can't go wrong. There are three faint maintenance paths off to the left accessing inspection huts along the pipe bringing water from the spring to the village, but the route is never in doubt as we follow beautifully graded traverses for almost two kilometres, until we come to a bend in a surfaced branch of the **Cami de la Rabosa** (Wp.21 246M), where we bear left to stay on the path down to Wp.2.

The classic ascent of the **Castellet de Castell de Castells** (aka **Castell de la Serrella**) via the **PR149**, with one small divergence to avoid walking the same path twice. Apart from the spur onto the summit, easy walking throughout with superb views, in particular a glorious perspective on the wilder mountains to the west. A great half-day outing, leaving plenty of time for indulging in the very decent Menu del Dia at the **Restaurant Hierbas** in the centre of **Castell de Castells**. Once you've seen the location of the castle, you'll understand the village's name. The castle of castles it is or was: there's not much of it left now, but until the seventeenth century this was a vital strategic outpost controlling the valleys flanking **La Serrella**.

Vertigo warning (only applicable to the branch climbing to the summit).

Access: Castell de Castells is located at the head of the **Vall de Pop** at the intersection of the CV752 from **Tarbena** and the CV720 from **Pedreguer**. The walk starts from the **El Castellet** *area recreativa y zona de acampada*, which lies to the south of the CV752, 250 metres east of the junction with CV720. The surfaced access track is marked by two brown signs for 'El Castellet' and a **PR149** fingerpost. The track is metalled with tarmac for the first 100 metres, thereafter with concrete. We park among the trees above the facility block 500 metres from the road, where there is a map board outlining our itinerary and a PR fingerpost indicating the track we take to the southwest.

Setting off on the dirt track to the southwest (Wp.1 0M), we climb between a small pine wood and terraces of olive trees, the castle summit and the track we follow across the face of the mountain both clearly visible above us. 475 metres from the parking area, the PR forks left at a clearly waymarked junction (Wp.2 10M), but we carry straight on, staying on the dirt track until it ends 75 metres later at the last of the cultivated terraces.

From the last of the terraces a narrow, unmarked but clear path climbs across abandoned terracing, initially in a westerly direction (Wp.3). After nearly 500 metres of steady but well graded climbing, we rejoin the PR on the dirt track seen from below (Wp.4 29M). We now follow the PR for the rest of the walk. Directly ahead of us, the narrow path continues to climb straight up, but there is little purpose in following it, as it cuts out some of the best bits of the itinerary. Turning right towards the rough ridge of the **Aspres de Famorca**, we enjoy 1500 metres of a beautiful balcony track, with fine views over **Castell de Castells** and the bare, humped back of the **Serra d'Alfaro** (Walk 37). At a junction with a broader track climbing from the CV720 (Wp.5 49M 2.7km), we bear left and climb steadily to reach the crest west of **El Castellet**, where views open out over the **Guadalest** valley to the south, **Aitana** to the southwest (Walks 7 & 10), and **Aixorta** to the east (Walks 18 & 20) (Wp.6 65M).

.. dramatic scar of the Barranc de la Canal ..

Immediately to our right, behind the **Aspres de Famorca**, we can see the dramatic scar of the **Barranc de la Canal** couloir (Walk 16). The track narrows here, but the walking remains easy as we skirt the summit of the **Alto de Tronca** then descend (E) toward a col, on the right of which we can see a half-moon threshing circle (the **Era del Rallat**) beside a small Moorish ruin, the **Pou del Frare**. The track bottoms out at an intersection (Wp.7 76M 4.6km) with the path climbing from Wp.4 and a spur track off to our right leading to the **Pou del Frare**. Sticking to the main track, we climb to a signpost (Wp.8 89M), behind which a narrow path climbs steeply (SW) to a cistern in the

the signpost at Wp.8

El Castellet seen from the east

outer defences of the castle (Wp.9 95M). At the cistern, the path veers right to reach a rough occasionally vertiginous way weaving through the rocks to the southeast to reach the summit, now a bastion of sheep, who have liberally carpeted the place with their droppings (Wp.10 102M).

For all that, it's a fabulous little eyrie and well worth the climb, though not when the rocks are wet, and great care should be taken at any time, since there are a couple of spots where a fall would be fatal.

Returning to the track (112M), we zigzag down to a crossroads at the **Portet de Castells** pass (Wp.11 125M). The **PR150** (Walk 18) continues directly ahead of us. On the right, the PRs 18 & 19 climb from **Guadalest**, though since these last two routes are surfaced for the first eight kilometres, they are effectively redundant as far as hiking is concerned. Turning left, we descend on concrete for a couple of hundred metres then, 50 metres above a square reservoir, turn left again, this time on a dirt track (Wp.12 130M). 550 metres later, the track swings left, bringing the **Aspres de Famorca** back into view, at which point we turn right on a signposted path (Wp.13 139M) for a straightforward descent to rejoin our outward route at Wp.2 (154M).

A fine walk to the summit of the **Serra de Aixorta**, picking the very best bits from three **PRs** (**18**, **150**, & **151**) and adding a few bits of my own to make a single long circuit. After the **Serra Forada** (Walk 25), the **Arcs de Castell de Castells** are the most famous limestone arches in the region, and well worth a visit, even if you don't feel up to the full itinerary, hence the alternative approach of the stroll. The boys from the blackstuff have got to the traditional Arcs route of the **PR151**, but not all the way, and this short stretch ends at a sight so very compelling, a whole lot more tarmac couldn't spoil the spectacle. The exertion rating on the main walk is only for sheer length and the steep climb at the top. Otherwise, easy walking, almost entirely on dirt tracks. There are two brief stretches offpath (see Wps. 13 & 21), both of which can be avoided if you don't like the look of them. The **Restaurant Hierbas** in the centre of **Castell de Castells** does a very decent *Menu del Dia*, though you'd have to be up very early in the morning to knock this one off in time for lunch.

4 | 5H 30M | 20.8 km | 845m / 845m | ↻ | 4

Access: Castell de Castells is located at the head of the **Vall de Pop** at the intersection of the CV752 from **Tarbena** and the CV720 from **Pedreguer**. Immediately south of the village, we take the *Centre Urba* turning off the CV720 then park 50 metres later in the large car park on the left behind the *Consultorio* and above the **Carnisseria Miquel**.

From the car park entrance (Wp.1 0M), we take the narrow road off to the right, **Calle de Ramon Rubial**, which joins the CV752 350 metres later (Wp.2 6M).

Turning left, we pass the lane up to the **El Castellet** *area recreativa* (brown sign) and take the second turning on the right, a concrete track, also signposted 'El Castellet' (off-white sign), where there's a mapboard for the **PRs 18** & **19**, and a fingerpost for the route we follow throughout most of the climb, the **PR150 Morro Blau** (Wp.3).

Apart from one brief break, the track is concreted for the first 400 metres, after which we continue on a good, well-stabilized dirt track, a small conical peak visible off to our left, which we will pass behind a little under five kilometres later. We pass two very minor forks to the left before coming to a third, much broader fork, where a hunting plaque has had the letters 'EE' painted on its back, and we can see off to our left a long, low house roofed with red tiles (Wp.4 26M). The left branch here is our return route. The track is readily drivable to this point, a little under 1.3km from the road, and there is room for two cars to park at the junction if you prefer to cut the initial climb. For the present, we continue climbing on the main track, ignoring a minor branch on

El Castellets comes into view

the left, after which we can see the rocky rise of **El Castellet** (Walk 17) and the dip of the **Portet de Castells** where the **PR150** is joined by the **PR18** from **Guadalest**. As we approach the *portet*, we pass a small firefighting reservoir, where the concrete resumes and we briefly intersect with Walk 17. The concrete ends at a crossroads on the near side of

the *portet* (Wp.5 53M 3.5km) and we turn left on a dirt track signposted 'R18 Cumbre Aixorta'.

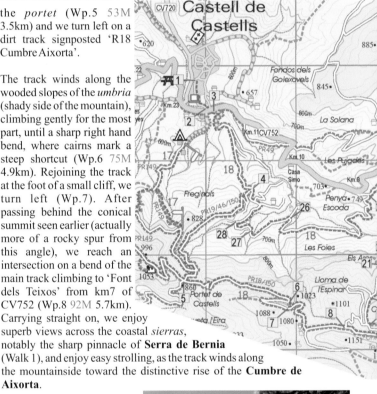

The track winds along the wooded slopes of the *umbria* (shady side of the mountain), climbing gently for the most part, until a sharp right hand bend, where cairns mark a steep shortcut (Wp.6 75M 4.9km). Rejoining the track at the foot of a small cliff, we turn left (Wp.7). After passing behind the conical summit seen earlier (actually more of a rocky spur from this angle), we reach an intersection on a bend of the main track climbing to 'Font dels Teixos' from km7 of CV752 (Wp.8 92M 5.7km). Carrying straight on, we enjoy superb views across the coastal *sierras*, notably the sharp pinnacle of **Serra de Bernia** (Walk 1), and enjoy easy strolling, as the track winds along the mountainside toward the distinctive rise of the **Cumbre de Aixorta**.

Down to the left, we can see the traces of a faint track which we use for our descent. One kilometre short of the **Font dels Teixos** (according to the official sign), we come to a Y-junction (Wp.9 114M 7.5km). The left hand branch is the start of our descent, but for the present, we carry straight on along the right

Cumbre de Aixorta

hand fork. The track soon passes a firefighting reservoir, after which it's concreted again for the final approach to the **Font dels Teixos**, below which we come to another Y-junction (Wp.10 124M 8.2km). The **PR18 Cumbre de Aixorta** forks right here, the **PR150 Morro Blau** left.

the refuge at
Font dels Teixos

We follow the former round to the right into the **Font dels Teixos** *area recreativa*, where there is a small refuge (unlocked or very possibly door-less depending on whether they get round to replacing the sheet of plastic that currently serves that purpose) and the eponymous font, which gives forth a rather meagre trickle and ought not to be relied upon.

Directly behind the refuge, a broad path crosses a stand of pine, narrowing to a rocky way traversing open scrub toward a mini-col behind the summit. At the col, a PR cross (Wp.11 132M) indicates where we bear right on a rough, well waymarked way climbing steeply to the summit cairn on the **Cumbre de Aixorta** (Wp.12 144M) (aka **Cerro de los Parados** or **Penya Alta**). Off to the east is the firewatch hut on the summit of **Morro Blau**, the objective of the **PR150**. Taking care on the loose stones, we retrace our steps to Wp.11, where we can either return to Wp.10 via the same route, or, if you don't object to a brief stretch of off-path walking, carry straight on, following a narrow path down toward the level, tilled land of the **Foia de Font Major**, a *foia* being a shallow mountain valley. The path peters out on the edge of the fields (Wp.13 156M), but we simply bear left, skirting the fields on an infinitely faint trodden way (effectively off path, though the walking is easy) to join the **Morro Blau** track at the bottom of the last stretch of concrete (Wp.14 159M).

Having already visited the higher summit, there's little advantage to be had from scaling **Morro Blau**, so we turn left here, then left again at the next junction (Wp.15) to return first to Wp.10 (174M) then Wp.9 (183M). As you approach **Font dels Teixos**, look over to your right to the **Alts del Cocoll**, where you'll see the rather extraordinary sight of a roller-coaster runway!

At Wp.9, we double back to the right, descending toward the **Sacanyar** valley, ignoring a branch off to the right 175 metres lower down (Wp.16). When the track swings sharp right 500 metres later (Wp.17 193M), we turn left on a very rough track crossing a terraced rise and a dry watercourse, beyond which it is so badly eroded it barely resembles a track at all. A brief climb brings us to a junction with a bend of a marginally better preserved track at the **Colladet de Sardina** (Wp.18 210M 13km).

Turning right, we descend through a pleasantly shady pine wood to join a concreted stretch of the main **Font dels Teixos** track (Wp.19 215M), where we turn right. The concrete ends after 200 metres, at which point, if you look down to your left, you will see a track snaking down into a valley. This is the **Cami de les Foies**, which we take when we leave the **PR151** at Wp.25. Another 300 metres, brings us to a second stretch of concrete, which ends immediately after a sharp right hand bend 200 metres later. We leave the track just before the end of this second stretch of concrete, on the cusp of the bend, turning left on a narrow path marked with a large blue dot, a black 'C' and an arrow (Wp.20 234M). 50 metres later, we fork right (Wp.21) to reach a superb natural *mirador* overlooking **Els Arcs**, at which point we have a choice of routes.

If you don't fancy rough off path walking, albeit only for about 100 metres, return to the main track and follow it down till the concrete gives way to asphalt, at which point, turn left, joining the stroll at Wp.2 and the full itinerary 300 metres later at Wp.23.

Otherwise, it is possible to descend directly to **Els Arcs**. Crossing the rocks immediately beyond the mirador (carefully, there's a nasty little drop off to the right), we rejoin the path we left at Wp.21 and follow it round the head of the slope between the *mirador* and **Els Arcs**.

Els Arcs

On the far side of the slope, we double back to the right and pick our way across the scrub, descending laterally directly below the cliffs of the *mirador* (off path) to join the **PR151** about 50 metres to the right of the arches themselves (Wp.22 243M).

Bearing right, we follow the PR151 toward a band of terracing, where the path broadens to a narrow track, leading to a signposted junction with another track (Wp.23 251M). This is Wp.3 of the stroll, which is where you will rejoin us if you opted to descend via the main track. If you're approaching via the stroll, carry straight on here, if you're arriving from **Els Arcs**, turn left, in both cases following the sign for 'Penya Escoda'. After passing a recently reconstructed house, we come to another signposted junction, where we again turn left for the 'Penya Escoda', following one of the spurs of the **PR151** (Wp.24 258M), at the end of which, we will leave the waymarked itinerary.

The track we used for the ascent comes into view as we approach the **Penya Escoda**, an undistinguished little hump of rock directly above the CV752, remarkable chiefly for a mapboard and the fact that we ignore the fingerpost's suggestion that we go back the way we've just come. Directly behind the *penya*, a partially concreted track descends on the right to the road, but we turn left on the **Cami de les Foies** (Wp.25 264M 15.8km), a narrow dirt track snaking down into the **Foies** valley. Although it's not immediately evident as we descend, this is a double-headed valley and as we wind into the second 'head', an interesting and unusual perspective opens upon the **Arcs** above us. At a junction with a slightly broader track (Wp.26 287M), we fork left, passing a couple of terrace access tracks. Ignoring a rough branch climbing to the left (Wp.27 294M) and a concreted branch on the left 200 metres after that (Wp.28), we stick to the main track until it rejoins our outward route at Wp.4 (304M 19.1km).

Els Arcs stroll

Access: From km7 of the CV752 between **Tarbena** and **Castell de Castells**, take the broad, well-stabilized track to the south, signposted 'Font dels Teixos 9km'. There is also a mapboard for the **PR151**. After 600 metres, the track becomes an asphalted lane drive very slowly here, the road is striated with drainage humps, most of which are unmarked and could happily take the sump out of your hire car if you hit them at speed. We park 800 metres later, in the large parking area on the left at a sharp right hand bend.

From the car park (Wp.1 0M), we continue on foot along the lane for another 600 metres until the tarmac runs into concrete, at which point we turn right on a dirt track for 'Penya Escoda, Els Arcs' (Wp.2 10M).

Just over 300 metres later, we fork left for 'Els Arcs' (Wp.3 14M) and follow an attractive track across almond terraces, where it dwindles to a path leading to the arches a little over 350 metres later (Wp.4 25M). We return the same way.

Bad news first. The **Font dels Olbis** is a bit shabby and barely merits a mention, let alone a walk named after it, there's too much tarmac and concrete track on the **PR145**, the waymarking is a bit iffy, and some kind soul has gone round removing all the signs from the posts. Naturally, the removal of the signposts made me all the more determined to do the walk and I'm glad I did, for the good news readily outweighs the bad. First, we get to visit a lovely valley that has beguiled weekenders, holidaymakers, and expats for decades, second we feast our eyes on the magnificent **Serra del Ferrer**, third we traverse a gratifyingly wild rockscape, fourth we get some stunning views, and fifth we end with a path so perfect that the Virgin Mary Herself might have conceived it had She not been busy elsewhere. **Parelles** is the rockscape in the lee of the **Serra del Carrascal de Parcent** near **Font dels Olbis**, **Serrals** the valley we circle at the end. The official title of the PR puts **Serrals** before **Parelles**, implying the walk should be done the other way round, but an anticlockwise circuit avoids a 200 metre climb at the end and saves the best bit for last. There's one stretch (Wps.13 - 16) where we diverge from the PR for reasons explained in the text. Unless the signposts are repaired and the waymarking redone, I'm afraid a certain amount of time consulting the book en route is inevitable for non-GPS users. Happily, though the last kilometre features so many turnings that it reads like a description of a circuit diagram, it's well waymarked and relatively easy to follow.

Short Version: if you don't want to do the full circuit, the best bit of the route can be reached as follows. From Wp.1, when the **Avinguda d'Eusebio Signes** starts to descend back to the CV715, fork left, passing to the right of the mapboard 75 metres later. Follow the concrete track up to the junction at the yellow house on the hill (Wp.31), then bear right to reach a bend in the CV752. Immediately to the left are three tracks, the third of which (waymarked with a red dot) leads to Wp.24.

the monument at Wp.1

Access: Tarbena lies on the CV715, midway between **Callosa d'en Sarria** and **Parcent**. Immediately south of km40 of the CV715, at the western end of **Tarbena**, we take **Avinguda d'Eusebio Signes** to the south and park in the large car park on the right 100 metres later beside the monument to the Mallorcan settlers who re-colonized the village when the Moriscos were expelled.

From the monument (Wp.1 0M), we return to the CV715 and walk up the road, passing the km40 sign and the junction with the CV752, 40 metres after which, we fork right on a narrow concrete track in front of the Autotaller Soliman garage (Wp.2 8M). Descending to a junction at the **Font de Benissalim** where the concrete track doubles back to the left, we fork right on a broad grassy path running along a contour line (Wp.3 16M). We soon resume our descent into the **Foia del Sabaig** valley, traces of ancient cobbling appearing on the path. Reaching a Y-junction (Wp.4 22M), we carry straight on along the right hand fork, heading toward the **Casa Lehmi** hotel, the large yellow building below us in the middle of the valley. After crossing a cherry orchard, our trail becomes a narrow concrete track, at the end of which, we ignore a minor lane doubling back to the right, and turn right on the main lane passing in front of the **Casa Lehmi** (Wp.5 35M 1.9km).

traditional cane rafters

Immediately after the hotel, we fork left at a Y-junction (Wp.6 37M), climbing steadily and passing several houses, including the **Villa Nieve**, shortly after which, the porch of the old house on the right has a well preserved example of the cane rafters that were once the standard ceilings in most Spanish cottages.

When the lane levels out (Wp.7 47M), we turn left on a concrete track and immediately fork right, ignoring the dirt track that doubles back to the left. Climbing steeply, we pass directly behind a small house and a ruin, just after which we come to a Y-junction (Wp.8 51M). Carrying straight on along the right hand fork, we pass behind a terrace of almond trees and enter a small pine wood patched with olive groves.

the house above km37

When the path doubles back to the left, we ignore a minor branch on the right (Wp.9 55M) and continue climbing along the broader trail until it joins another narrow concrete track (Wp.10 59M 3.5km). Turning right, we follow this track all the way to the CV715 (Wp.11 67M), at which point we turn left to walk along the road for 600 metres.

When the road swings sharp left to pass below a small house with one brick red wall, about 100 metres before km37, we double back to the right, on yet another narrow concrete track, climbing alongside a fenced orchard (Wp.12 75M 4.4km). The track climbs to a junction abreast of two small houses (Wp.13 81M), at which point we're confronted with a bit of a poser. The PR is meant to bear right here onto an obscure path climbing directly behind the house alongside the **Barranc del Pas**, but somebody has painted a PR cross at the mouth of the turning. Whether this is official or just a jeu d'esprit on the part of the householder, I wouldn't know, but in the absence of any other waymarked route and to avoid any potential unpleasantness, I propose the following alternative.

Bearing left and ignoring another branch on the right a few metres later, we stick to the main track, climbing steadily across successive stretches of concrete, passing a *caseta* and skirting terraces of olive trees. 850 metres after the dubious cross, the track approaches terraces of almond trees, where it appears to end. In fact, it doubles back to the left before ending at a bricked up cabin, but we don't want to go there! Just before the track doubles back to the left, we fork right (Wp.14 96M), following a trodden way onto a terrace and immediately descend onto a grassy path running along the terrace directly below. This attractive path gradually broadens to a trail following a contour line (E then NE) before veering left at a large boulder above a second almond grove (Wp.15 100M), and climbing (W) to rejoin the official route of the PR at a junction with a cairn-marked path on the right (Wp.16 102M 5.9km).

Hereon in, pathfinding is not a problem and the waymarks are more frequent, though they do not appear at every vital junction. Carrying straight on, we climb along a broad stony trail, passing two ruins, after which the trail becomes a track, passing in front of the **Font dels Olbis** (Wp.17 108M 6.5km) and behind a small brick house that has been visible through much of the climb from the road. We follow this track all the way down to the CV752, ignoring a branch doubling back to the right near the top (Wp.18 113M) and another turning on the right at a concreted junction toward the bottom (Wp.19 125M), enjoying superb views throughout.

When the track reaches the road (Wp.20 128M 8km), we bear left and follow the road for 130 metres, then fork right twice in 25 metres (Wp.21 130M), first onto a newly asphalted track, then onto a well-stabilized dirt track. We follow the dirt track down toward the **Barranc de les Viudes**, turning left at a T-junction (Wp.22 140M) to descend for another couple of hundred metres, after which a long gentle climb brings us to a point where the track has been surfaced (Wp.23 146M). We now have another long stretch on tarmac, which would be utterly tedious were it not for the fact that the **Serrals** valley soon comes into view and we see, down to our right, the fabulous little path that is in many ways the highlight of this itinerary.

One kilometre after the start of the tarmac, one too many, but probably worth it for what we are about to embark on, we double back to the right on a broad cairn and waymarked path (Wp.24 159M).

the 'smile' after **Wp.24**

This beautiful path curls around above the **Serrals** valley, overlooking the broad smile (you'll see what I mean when you're at the head of the valley) of the dirt track that we take back toward **Tarbena**. On the far side of the valley, our path swings round to the left and we descend past a ruin to a junction with a narrower path off to the left leading to the dirt track we saw from above (Wp.25 176M).

Rather than turning left directly, we carry straight on here and bear round to the right to a superb natural *mirador* overlooking the **Algar** cliffs.

the Algar cliffs

Sated with views, we retrace our steps to the head of the dirt track and descend into the **Serrals** valley, on the far side of which the track runs into concrete at a junction with a spur doubling back to the right. 50 metres up the concrete, we fork right (Wp.26 186M), turning left 40 metres after that (Wp.27) and immediately forking right on a narrow path running along a terrace to pass directly in front of a small cabin. Continuing along a narrow terrace (SE), we bear left above a small well (Wp.28 192M) on a partially concreted path climbing to cross a dirt track (Wp.29 195M), ten metres above which, we turn left on a concrete track (Wp.30). At the intersection of concrete tracks 50 metres later (Wp.31), we bear right to return to our starting point.

Serendipity played its part in our discovery of **Serra del Raco Roig**, the Sierra of the Red Corner, a satellite range in the northern foothills of **Serra de Aixorta**. Toward the end of our researches, I was checking the distribution of the walks we had done and realized there was a gap in the **Bolulla** region. A bit of hard staring at maps and mountains suggested this might be a feasible itinerary, so we set off not really knowing what to expect, if anything at all, which was slightly insane since we had recently done three very tough walks that got rejected as being undesirable.

As it turned out, the itinerary was already waymarked (immaculately, it must be said, congratulations to whoever did the work) and proved a triumph, taking us into a beautiful, barren landscape, in which the exquisite vies with the majestic, conjuring an atmosphere that had me humming the old blues lyric about being 'a thousand miles from nowhere'. For the bluesmen, it was an image of lonesome melancholia, but to my mind it always seemed like a very good place to be, and the **Serra del Raco Roig** is a very good place to be, indeed. In short, a fine walk with one or two moments of quite surpassing wonder. The path is rough in places, but on the whole the walking is very easy. Take plenty of water, though. The northern flank of the mountain is very bleak and bare and would be absolute murder on a hot day without enough water. The risk of vertigo is very, very slight, but worth mentioning.

Access: Bollulla lies on the CV715 between **Callosa d'en Sarria** and **Tarbena**. 700 metres north of **Bolulla**, on the cusp of the hairpin bend at km45.6 of the CV715, we take the unnumbered road to the north, which at the time of writing is marked by a sign advertizing 'O.I.H. Urbana'. We park in the broad bend of the track at the end of the tarmac 3.6 kilometres later 3.6 very impressive kilometres it must be said, as the road climbs toward the cliffs of the **Riu Algar** gorge, the **Penya del Castellet**, and the ruins of **Castell de Garx**.

From the end of the tarmac (Wp.1 0M), we continue along the dirt track, passing between an attractive stone house and a ruin to approach the col behind **Castell de Garx**. Just short of the col, a large cairn and red and orange arrows on a rock on our left indicate the narrow path we take along the southern flank of **Raco Roig** (Wp.2 7M).

waypoint 2

That's pretty much all you need to know for the next kilometre and a half, as the ongoing path is clear and unmistakable all the way to the top of the **Barranc de la Serra** (aka **Barranc de la Canal Negre**), the ravine off to our left, which deepens and becomes more clearly defined the higher we climb. So just sit back, or rather step forward, and enjoy the sounds of silence, a silence so deep that even the soughing of the wind can sound loud in your ears.

Apart from that, the only noises you can expect to hear are the chirpings of crickets and birds and the occasional drone of a distant airplane, the latter eliciting one of those delicious moments of schadenfreude for anybody who has ever peered out of a plane window and thought, "That looks interesting down there. I don't want to be up here. I want to be down there". We are!

Passing a ruined corral 100 metres from the track, we climb gently across broad, long abandoned terracing, bringing into view (up to our left) the roof of the **Morro Blau** firewatch hut and the **Cumbre de Aixorta** (Walk 18). For the most part, the only evidence that we are climbing at all is the deepening ravine on our left, though shortly after passing a second ruined corral (Wp.3 25M), the path does veer round to the right and climb more steadily for about 100 metres before the easier gradient reasserts itself. At the head of the ravine, the terraces become broader and grassier, and we pass a very faint, overgrown, cairn-framed path climbing to the left (Wp.4 52M 2km).

Carrying straight on, following the clearer stretches of path and the occasional red arrow, we cross a small stand of pine, beyond which our path descends into the **Barranc de Sacanyar** (Wp.5 57M), from where we can see off to the right the orange tiled roof of a small house, which is where our return route begins. At the deep retaining wall at the head of the ravine (Wp.6 60M), we ignore a faint path off to the left and turn right to follow a contour line along the left bank of the ravine. The path dips into a patch of holm oak 50 metres later, after which we're greeted by the astonishing sight of the **Arc dels Xorquets**, an incredibly fine and delicately fashioned window in the wall of rock on the far side of the gully. Ignoring a very faint branch on the left (Wp.7

El Arc dels Xorquets

66M), we continue along the main path, soon traversing a rough, rocky stretch (watch where you put your feet), after which the path flattens out on an old terrace and runs into the end of a dirt track (Wp.8 74M 3km). We follow the track until it debouches into the parking area of the **Els Arcs** stroll (Walk 18) and joins an asphalted stretch of the **Font dels Teix** track (Wp.9 80M).

Turning right, we follow the road for 200 metres, then turn right again on a dirt track (Wp.10 83M), to 'PR151 Aljib Xorquet', an *aljib* or *aljub* being a reservoir of Arabic origin. Though you wouldn't know it from the waymarkings, this is also part of the **PR49** between **Callosa d'en Sarria** and **Castell de Castells**, which we follow back to the **Castell de Garx** col.

Forking right immediately after the turning (the left fork is the **PR151** to the *aljub*), we ignore a PR cross a couple of hundred metres later (Wp.11) and a turning on the right 30 metres after that (Wp.12 87M). When the main track doubles back to the left (Wp.13 92M), we bear right on a broad trail skirting an almond grove, beyond which the trail dwindles to a narrow path, and the duties of a walking guide also dwindle somewhat, as we embark on another 'that's all you really need to know' stretch of the walk, the path from here to the end being narrow, but unequivocal. Climbing slightly alongside the **Barranc de la Cova Roja** (aka **Barranc del Xorquet**), we soon see the eponymous cave on the far side of the ravine. We then traverse the broad, bare slopes of **La Foia del Clot**, where we pass a very ruinous ruin (Wp.14 111M) that is emblematic of the landscape here, much of which must once have been pasture but has now become dessicated scrub.

the Algar gorge

Beyond the ruin, we cross a small rise (worth pausing as you climb to look back for a fine view of **Barranc de la Canal** Walk 16) and curve round to the south, an extraordinary spectacle unfolding before our eyes, one in which the **Serras del Ferrer** and **Bernia** are reduced to mere backdrops for the dramatic cliffs and convolute rock formations above the **Algar** gorge, which some maps mark as **Pas Tancat**, literally 'closed pass' you can see what they were getting at.

The path scarcely loses ground at all until toward the end and then only gently, passing one very brief stretch where there is an infinitesimally slight risk of vertigo (most people won't even notice it). Thereafter, an intermittently stepped descent brings us to a shady hanger of pine where we pick our way through the debris of a dramatic and dramatically fresh rockspill (Wp.15 140M), 200 metres after which we rejoin the dirt track at the **Castell del Garx** col, just short of Wp.2 (144M).

The **La Safor** mountains can look a little monotonous from afar, but once you get into them (and we get way into them on this walk), they are anything but. In fact, parts of this itinerary could do with being a bit more monotonous. The route is a variant of the **PR42 Ruta de Josep Mascarell**, climbing from **Orxa** to the rim of the fabulous **Circ de la Safor** before returning via the equally phenomenal **Riu Serpis** ravine (aka **Barranc de l'Infern**). If you recall, in the introduction, I drew an analogy between certain Costa Blanca PRs and a Brazilian bikini. This was the walk I had in mind when I made the comparison, for though there are several decent paths, a long stroll on a good dirt track, and even a bit of road walking, the main climb is in the hoof-steps of goats who aren't much given to coherent path-making, while the descent involves tunnelling through shoulder high holm oak and traversing jagged limestone on precipitous trails that are so infinitesimal one begins to suspect they were made by wild animals and are shortly going to disappear altogether, leaving us floundering about on all fours hoping the hunters don't mistake us for something palatable. It doesn't quite come to that, but there were moments when I found myself wondering who the hell was Josep Mascarell and what sort of lunatic would pioneer a route like this?

To be fair to him, Josep Mascarell may never have walked these paths at all. He was a local writer who championed the regional railway links when the dictates of economics declared them redundant. It is, therefore, entirely possible that the naming of the PR was merely commemorative, since the stretch in the ravine follows the **Raco del Duc**, the former railway line linking the industrial hinterland with the coast, a line that was also known as *el tren de los ingleses*, since it was developed and exploited by the Alcoy & Gandia Railways and Harbour Company Ltd which would be a lot less snappy as an itinerary title.

So, tough, rough, steep, hard to follow, touched by lunacy . . . and, of course, the most tremendous fun, too, something which, if you are still reading, you are probably of a temperament to have deduced already. The views from the top are sublime, the ravine is an exhilarating poem in rock, water, and oleander, the sense of a grand adventure is quite overpowering, the paths are every bit as astonishing as they are punishing, and I wouldn't mind betting you'll end the day thinking, "By God, that was good, I want to go back and do it all again." However, it is still a walk that, perversely, I feel duty bound to discourage people from doing! The Brazilian Bikini after Wp.16 could very well be some walkers' definition of hell, and even those who love this sort of thing would be well advised to come well clad if they don't want to be shredded. We were wearing shorts and I bear the scars to this day, some three months later! Enough, though. If it's for you, you'll know already; and if it's not for you, there's still the option of the Short Versions, which should suit most dispositions. The **Raco del Duc** is a must do in one form or another.

Apart from being mad, bad, and dangerous to follow, the only drawback to the **PR42** is that it begins with a wearisome climb on four kilometres of very unnecessary tarmac. To avoid this, we start on the **PR207 Ruta de los Fuentes**, which we also use for our descent into the ravine.

Vertigo warning: at no point do we risk dropping off a cliff, not unless we go out of our way to do so, but the descent involves a dizzying, bird's eye view that might trigger certain varieties of vertigo.

Short versions

(a) Taken from the bridge over the **Serpis** at Wp.31, the **Raco del Duc** is ideal for anything from a short stroll to a long linear walk (up to 20 kilometres counting the return). It can also be accessed (on signposted tracks) from the coast via the quarry 3.5km west of **Villalonga**, though in that case it's best to take a torch as the first tunnel is quite long.

(b) Font dels Olbits 3h / 8.5km (estimated time and distance). From Wp.11 take the dirt track out of the *area recreativa* to join the road traversing **La Safor** some 500 metres later. Turn left, then left again about 10 minutes later on a track signposted 'Font dels Bassiets 2.7km'. The track passes below two new corrals after 800 metres, rejoining our outward route at Wp.7 600 metres later.

(c) PR207 4h30 / 14.7km (official time and distance). As per short version b, from Wp.11 take the dirt track to reach the road traversing **La Safor**. Turn right to reach Wp.23 about 10 minutes later, then turn left to follow the remainder of the walk as described.

Access: Orxa is at the end of the CV701, which can be reached via the CV705 from the north (**Rugat**) and south (**Alcoi**), or the CV711 off the **Vall de Gallinera** road (the CV700) if you're based on the coast. Either way, do not drive into the village itself. It's a labyrinth of narrow one-way alleys. Arriving on the CV701, we cross a road bridge over the **Riu Serpis**, on the near side of which is the access to **Raco del Duc**. After the bridge, we stay on the tail end of the CV701 alongside a dry, concreted riverbed, carrying straight on at a roundabout and passing a turning doubling back to the right. Thereafter, the road widens before reaching a second, broader right hand turn where there is plentiful roadside parking. There are no street names or road signs here, but the turning is just before **Orxa** industrial park, which consists principally of a paper treatment plant and the Marcelino Bonastre Fabrica de Tejidos.

the mapboard at the start (Wp.1)

The walk starts on the other side of the road immediately after the broad turning, opposite a Telefonica substation, on a dirt track where there's a mapboard for the **PR207** (Wp.1 0M). Heading east, we follow the track alongside the dry torrent of **Barranc de Vessant**.

After 350 metres, we reach a dam wall, where a PR signpost indicates that we descend to the left, directly behind the dam, into the bed of the torrent (Wp.2 5M). The path in the streambed is faint, but readily deduced so long as we bear in mind that our next objective is the **Cova de Gregori**, the large cave clearly visible up to our left.

75 metres after the dam (Wp.3), we ignore ways climbing to left and right, and stay in the streambed for another 100 metres before forking right (Wp.4) on a rough path along the left bank (our right) of the stream. 150 metres later, we descend back into the streambed directly in front of the cave (Wp.5 16M), crossing onto the right bank five metres later. Following ancient blue splodges, rough PR waymarks, and the odd cairn, we climb across abandoned terraces, passing within ten metres of the cave, after which we follow a balcony path above the **Barranc de Vessant**, fine views opening up toward the **Safor** massif, including a rocky knoll up to the left, below which a cluster of pine trees mark the location of **Font dels Olbits**. Ignoring a minor fork to the left (Wp.6 29M), we climb on an increasingly broad and well made trail, passing to the right of a shallow slope of terraces sandwiched between two outcrops of rock. After a second balcony path, a steeper climb brings us to a concreted bend in the track leading to **Font dels Bassiets** (Wp.7 45M).

La Safor from Font dels Bassiets

Turning right, we descend to cross the watercourse at the confluence of the **Barrancs de la Carrasca** and **Bassiets**, which form the **Vessant**, at which point there's a 50 metre gap in the concrete. 75 metres after the concrete has resumed, ten metres before the track swings sharp right, we turn left (Wp.8 51M), on a narrow path, signposted 'Font dels Olbits 1.14 km 50M'.

After descending to the bed of a dry torrent, we climb to the right (Wp.9) momentarily dipping back into the torrent a couple of minutes later before continuing to climb along its left bank. For a while, we appear to be bypassing **Font dels Olbits** altogether, particularly when the trail becomes confused in a mishmash of goat paths, but following the main traces (NE) for 100 metres, we dip down to cross the bed of the torrent (Wp.10 68M) and double back to the left, heading towards **Olbits** (NW then N).

At the end of a contour line, views open out towards the distinctive pinnacle of **Benicadell**, and we zigzag up to the exquisite little *area recreativa* at **Font dels Olbits**, where the **PRs 42** and **207** intersect at the barbecue hut (Wp.11 79M). Turning right, now following the **PR42**, we climb the steps beside the barbecue hut, then turn right again a few metres later on the top terrace of the *area recreativa*.

the barbecue hut

The path, which is clear to begin with, promptly swings back toward the main rise of **La Safor** (NE), crossing patches of bare rock before reaching a shallow trench, where we continue across the bare rock, as indicated by waymarks, ignoring a goat path off to the left (Wp.12 85M), though the two ways merge 50 metres later. Maintaining a northeasterly direction on a mazy web of well-splintered goats' trails, we climb to an intersection with the end of a dirt track, where there's a small dew pond and an information board about the mountain's flora and fauna (Wp.13 94M). If you're beginning to feel this is looking a little too rough for your tastes (it gets an awful lot rougher), this track descends to the **Fonts dels Olbits** track. Otherwise, we carry straight on along a clearer trail, climbing in a more easterly direction, views opening out to the north over the dramatic rockscape framing the **Riu Serpis**.

Climbing steadily, we cross a runoff gully (Wp.14 106M), after which we zigzag up a steep stony path so rough that it's barely a path at all, only meriting the term by virtue of clarity. The oak become more abundant as the gradient gradually eases and the path skirts the northern flank of the mountain, from where we can glimpse, way below us, stretches of the **Riu Serpis** itself. Our way then winds back onto the central slope, approaching what appears to be the summit (it's not), at the foot of which we come to a reasonably distinct Y-junction (Wp.15 132M), where we fork right, sticking with the clearer traces traversing a shady stretch of oak. Crossing rough ground, but following a clear way, we wind through scrub and stunted oak, eventually emerging in a grassy dell, at the far end of which we pass a sinkhole and reach a signposted crossroads beside a snow gatherers' pit, the **Cava** or **Nevera de la Safor** (Wp.16 150M). The summit of **La Safor**, which we visit in Walk 22, is ten minutes to the right. Our ongoing itinerary is to the left. However, it's worth carrying straight on first for 75 metres to a superb natural *mirador* overlooking the **Circ de la Safor** cliffs.

Returning to Wp.16, we head north on a tiny path snaking through dense oak scrub to cross the ridge defining the dell, on the far side of which it looks like we're just going to drop off the edge of the mountain. We are! Though never manifestly risky, what ensues is quite extraordinary, only the occasional waymarks and scars of cut branches where the scrub has been trimmed suggesting that following this route is a sensible thing for a sane adult to do. Even then you may have your doubts. Quite apart from the path's minuscule dimensions (a large rucksack is a distinct liability amid the shoulder high oak), the way is very steep, very rough, and often a hands-on job. It's also worth noting that the rocks can be slippery. For many, it is a definitive nightmare. For others, a dream. You probably know who you are. Either way, take your time. We did. You won't want to be reading a book up here. Even consulting the GPS may seem a bit irksome. So, in brief, expect the following waystages on the descent:

La Finestra de la Safor (Wp.17)

- After a first painstaking descent, we cross a secondary rise and pass behind **La Finestra de la Safor** (Wp.17 169M).
- At the bottom of a long hands on stretch, we bear right at a waymarked junction (Wp.18 176M).

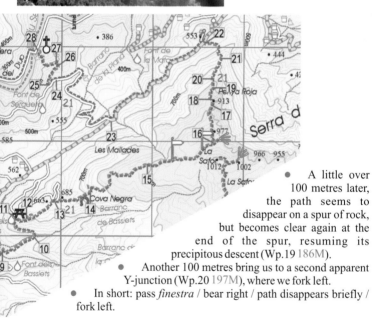

- A little over 100 metres later, the path seems to disappear on a spur of rock, but becomes clear again at the end of the spur, resuming its precipitous descent (Wp.19 186M).
- Another 100 metres bring us to a second apparent Y-junction (Wp.20 197M), where we fork left.
- In short: pass *finestra* / bear right / path disappears briefly / fork left.

A long, more northeasterly descent defined by a line of jagged limestone to our right brings us to a signposted junction with a narrow path doubling back to the left (Wp.21 212M), after which things become considerably easier. Directly below us, we can see a large square villa on the far side of the road. We will join the road in front of the gated track to the left of the villa. Ignoring the path doubling back to the left, we carry straight on and immediately descend to the left (N then W), following a less precipitous, but stony and skittery path down to the road (Wp.22 225M).

The **PR42** turns right here, but we turn left, following the road for 1.5km. This road used to be a nice dirt track, but after the antics of the preceding ninety minutes, the easy walking on sure footing isn't entirely unwelcome, especially since another wild little descent awaits us. After climbing (steadily but easily) out of a small dip, we rejoin the **PR207** at a junction with a dirt track on the right, signposted 'Font de Serquera' (Wp.23 243M). Apart from one minor fork to the right, there are no branches off this track until we reach the sign for the *area recreativa*, just above the installations themselves, so stash the book, stow the GPS, and enjoy the easy walking.

After passing a small, roofless ruin, the track describes a long hairpin and passes the minor fork off to the right (Wp.24 267M), beyond which superb views open out over the **Riu Serpis**. The main track then descends through a chicane directly above the *area recreativa*. Halfway through the chicane, at a large, battered, 'Medi Ambient' board, we turn right for 'Riu Serpis' / 'Finca de la Llum' (Wp.25 270M). The path that ensues is nothing compared to the descent off **La Safor**, but it is rough and often obscure. After following a contour line, we descend across a couple of abandoned terraces to approach a half metre high cairn perched on a rock (Wp.26 276M). Ignoring traces to the left of the cairn, we double back to the right, descending steeply into a wooded gully, already within sight of the railway line on the far bank of the river. The path winds back and forth before crossing bare rock below a dry spring (Wp.27 282M), after which we follow a contour line (W) toward a scattering of mature pine overlooking the roofless ruins of an outbuilding of the **Finca de la Llum**, the generating plant midway along the **Raco del Duc**. Beyond the pine, a clear but rough way zigzags down to pass between the roofless ruin and the generating plant's chapel, joining the **Raco del Duc** track (Wp.28 292M) 75 metres from the main ruin and the bridge over the **Serpis**.

Raco del Duc

Again, words and digital data are largely superfluous until we are within sight of **Orxa**, as we simply turn left, cross the river, and follow the track along the valley, marvelling at the magnificent ravine and enjoying a gentle end to a tough walk. Except for Wp.30, the following is merely for the purposes of pacing progress.

After 1.5km we pass a large roofless ruin (on our right) and a spur forking left to a weir (Wp.29 319M). A kilometre later, after we've been through a short tunnel and passed a large ivy clad ruin on the far bank of the river, we see a house backed by three tall cypress pine (**Casa Martin**), which is 2.5km from the road bridge over the **Riu Serpis**. 500 metres after the house we go through a cutting, the castle of **Perputxent** comes into view and the track veers right. 100 metres later, we turn sharp left (Wp.30 355M) on a minor track that traverses terraces toward the chimney stack of an old paper mill (SW) before bearing left to join the CV701 next to the road bridge (Wp.31 373M), where we turn left and follow the road back to the starting point.

For those who want to enjoy the glorious views from the **Circ de la Safor** without the hard work involved in Walk 21, this is the no frills version, a straightforward, linear gallop up to the summit and directly back down again. For all its simplicity, it's a fine walk, with good views throughout, and an agreeable sensation of isolation outside the weekends, the chances are that you'll be on your own up here, save for the bees buzzing about the bushy heather. The ground is rough underfoot and some care is required with pathfinding toward the top, but in every other respect, this is an easy walk following the end of the **Les Valls PR43**. Waymarking is poor at the start, but improves as we climb into wilder terrain.

Access: Depending on where you're based, the walk can be reached via the hamlet of **Llombai** in the **Vall de Gallinera** (off the CV700) or from **Orxa** (see Walk 21).

For the **Vall de Gallinera** access follow the CV700 to **Alpatro** (aka **Patro**) then, immediately west of the village, take the CV714 for **Benissili**. The **Orxa/Villalonga** road, which is unnumbered, unnamed and unsignposted (!), begins 100 metres west of **Llombai** in front of signs indicating that **Alpatro** and **Benissili** are 1km to the east and west. The upper zigzags of the road are clearly visible from the junction. The road climbs very steeply (you probably won't get above second gear for the first 1300 metres) then gradually levels out, passing the junction with the **Orxa** branch after 2km (signposted 'Centre BTT El Comtat'). 2.7km later, a wide, well stabilized, PR waymarked track comes in from the right. We can park on this track or in a large parking bay 50 metres along the marginally rougher track on the left 100 metres further along the road, where the trail to the summit begins.

If you're arriving from **Orxa**, simply carry on along the tail end of the CV701 after the access described in Walk 21 and turn left at the T-junction in the industrial park to reach the unnumbered road climbing to the **Centre BTT El Comtat** junction. Turn left to reach the starting point as described above.

From the wide track (Wp.1 0M), we walk up the road toward **Villalonga**, turning left 100 metres later toward the distant ruin of a corral (Wp.2 4M), already within sight of a clear trail snaking up the mountainside, which is the route we will join shortly.

the broad trail; the first part of the ascent

Descending along a stony track, we pass the parking bay mentioned in the access details, then skirt a small almond grove on a rough red track leading to a junction 300 metres from the road (Wp.3 9M), where we encounter our first PR waymarks.

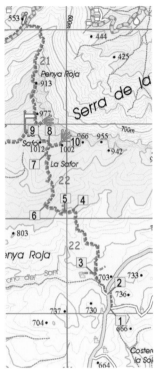

We turn right here then immediately fork left onto the trail we saw from the road.

Though often little more than a broad band of bare ground and sharp karst cutting a swathe through the scrub, the trail is perfectly clear in its lower reaches, climbing gently to steadily alongside an increasingly well defined gully toward a confluence of run-off channels. Just short of the confluence, the trail bears left, curving round the more westerly affluents, from where fine views open out behind us across the sierras to the south.

After passing under a small archway of holm oak, we veer left behind a shallow retaining wall (Wp.4 28M), crossing a second retaining wall to follow a contour line, bringing into view the mountains behind **Alcoi**. Forking left (Wp.5 31M) at a Y-junction with a minor branch to the right, on which there is a clear PR cross, we dip into the head of a second gully 100 metres later, where the trail dwindles to a path.

Weaving through dense banks of stunted oak, we climb to a rise, where the distinctive fist of **Benicadell** comes into view (Wp.6 38M) and we bear right to follow a more northerly trajectory on an increasingly rocky way, along which most of the oak give up their arboreal aspirations, resigning themselves to shrubdom. After levelling out for a while, our path drops into a dry swale, then climbs to a flat patch of coarse grass (Wp.7 59M), which in these parts might almost pass for a tiny pasture. Looking up to the left, we can see the trig point amid a cluster of small trees on the summit. 100 metres later, views open out over the coastal resorts to the north, and we come to a T-junction (Wp.8 62M). The **Cim de la Safor** is 100 metres to our left (Wp.9 65M), from where we have fine views toward **Villalonga** and as far north as the **Cullera** peninsula.

We return via the same route, taking care not to stray onto the PR waymarked path descending north to the snowpit on Walk 21. However, rather than turning right directly at Wp.8, I recommend carrying straight on for 150 metres, following the faint traces of an old path along the rim of the cirque to reach a fabulous natural *mirador* (Wp.10) with stunning views over the cliffs.

the plaque on the summit

Barranc de l'Encantada

For a one way walk that's barely longer than a stroll, we took a long time chipping away at the **Barranc de l'Encantada**, driving hither and thither, then walking hither and thither, often as not on the very roads we'd just hithered and thithered in the car. It was a bit galling, but it was worth 'wasting' the best part of two days in order to alert you to the splendours of this grand little gorge.

As far as I can work out with my very approximate Catalan, the *barranc* takes its name from a legend about a humble cottar being asked by a beautiful lady if he preferred her or her diamond necklace. The poor fool gets the answer wrong and both necklace and beauty promptly disappear into an enchanted palace up in the rocks. Touchy, I call it, but then these fairytale femme fatales were never known for their forbearance. Nonetheless, it really is an enchanting place, and it would merit the name even without some slighted beauty stalking off in a huff

Originally, we had hoped to piece together a circuit running the length of the gorge and looping back by one of the ridges, but this proved impossible, since the paths accessing the abandoned terraces at the northern end of the gorge, which should have made the traverse feasible, have all but disappeared, and nobody would thank us for dragging them through the invading scrub. However, the northern end is still worth visiting for a stroll and, in hot weather, perhaps a picnic under the poplars at the mouth of the *barranc*. It can be reached via the CV711 between **Beniarres** and **Planes**.

The **Barranc de l'Encantada** turning is a clearly signposted, single lane, surfaced track starting at the southern end of the **Embalse de Beniarres** dam wall. Park at the end of the tarmac 1.3 kilometres later, then take the track to the east to reach the terrace paths 250 metres later. From here, we can stroll along the streambed for about 100 metres or, climbing to the right, follow the western flank of the ravine for three hundred metres.

Due to the hither and thither business mentioned above, the time and distance are one way only.

Access: The walk is reached via the CV700 between **Pego** and **Muro de Alcoi**. A couple of kilometres east of **Planes**, immediately west of the **Calderes Bridge**, at km29 of the CV700, we take the surfaced track descending to the north. The track is indicated by a slightly peculiarly angled sign if you're approaching from the west, but there is no sign if you're coming from the east. However, it does have a 'BTT' cycling waypost and rough yellow and white waymarks, indicating a longer route coinciding with our

walk. 1200 metres later we pass **El Salt**, the imposing cliffs off to our right with improbably located graffiti striated across their midriff. 1500 metres from the road, we pass a track on the left beside a tiny house. We park 100 metres later in the layby on a bend above the streambed.

From the bend above the streambed (Wp.1 0M), we walk back to the tiny house and turn right on the track (Wp.2). 150 metres later, when the track goes through the wrought iron gates of **Villa Monica** (Wp.3 5M), we fork right on a broad trail, descending to a wide terraced field. Ignoring a minor fork on the left (Wp.4 8M), we continue along the edge of the field, passing a ruin above a small dam, below which we can see the first of the rockpools that are a feature of the *barranc*.

At the end of the field, the path continues to a Y-junction with a pine tree in the crux of the Y (Wp.5 13M). The two branches soon rejoin, but we take the minor fork to the right, descending past the pine. 50 metres after the two paths rejoin, we reach a ruined millhouse, the **Moli de la Encantada**, immediately after which we pass directly below a small spring and see, down to our right, the narrows known as the Clot del Moli. We then climb to a Y-junction directly below the ruins of a corral, where we fork left (Wp.6 20M), then left again 50 metres later (Wp.7).

Winding through cistus, broom and patches of pine, we soon see the line of mountains behind **Orxa**, which define the border between the provinces of **Valencia** and **Alicante**. When the path breaches the next rise, we glimpse the peak of **Benicadell** off to our left and get a superb outlook over the northern reaches of the gorge. Following a contour line, we pass a particularly fine strawberry tree (picked from the tree the fruits are bland, but those that have fallen or are about to fall can be intensely sweet), and approach a couple of tiny cabins in a fenced olive grove on the rim of the gorge. Immediately beyond the cabins, we join an eroded dirt track (Wp.8 35M 1.9km).

Climbing away from the cabins, we come to a junction with another surfaced track (Wp.9 38M) where the 'PR' (I'm not persuaded it's an official route and it certainly isn't desirable) turns left for a tedious traipse along tarmac. For our part, we simply turn right and follow the track (which is unsurfaced for the last 150 metres) to the north, enjoying fine views to the west, until we come to a small ruin on the right, which serves as a *mirador* looking back to the southern reaches of the gorge (Wp.10 40M 2.3km). We return by the same route.

The object of this walk was the subject of a pretty warm discussion . . .

She: "This is the best castle we've been to."

He: "Oh, no, Confrides was wilder."

She: "No, not like this, this is it."

He: "You can't compare."

She: "Really, it's true."

He: "I mean to say."

She: "Much better."

He: "Oh, come on!"

I'm sure you know the sort of thing I'm talking about. We got quite curt with one another for a while there. The scene wasn't as lively as in the thirteenth century, when the **Castillo de Alcala** (as it was known then) was the seat of Al-Azrac, the principal Moorish leader during the Christian re-conquest of Valencia, but it was a near thing. Bickering aside, it's a delightful walk, a perfect blend of the domestic and the wild, in the course of which you might begin to understand why legend holds that one Moorish prince claimed he didn't mind losing heritage, privilege, rank, wealth, title and power, but leaving **Vall de Gallinera** really broke his heart. As for the castle, I don't know . . . do Walk 7 as well and decide for yourselves which is 'better', but don't blame me if you and your partner disagree.

Access: We start from **Benissili**, the most westerly of the villages on the CV714, which loops off the main **Vall de Gallinera** road, the CV700, between km38.7, immediately west of Alpatro, and km36 east of the **Collado de Benissili**. The CV714 skirts the edge of **Benissili**, where it is (rather engagingly) called 'Carrer Carretera' i.e. Road Street. Immediately north of the road midway between the two 'Benissili Vall de Gallinera' signs, there is a small square lined with benches. We park in the concrete layby with a bottle bank to the right of this square.

From the car park (Wp.1 0M), we walk up **Road Street** for 50 metres, then turn right into an alley (Wp.2) marked with a 'Ruta dels 8 Pobles' plaque, a green and white waymarked *sendero local* that we follow until **Font de la Mata**. At the top of the steps at the end of the alley (Wp.3), we turn right then double back to the left on a delightful mule trail climbing toward the head of the valley. Turning left at a T-junction (Wp.4 12M), we follow a broader trail along a contour line onto a terrace, passing a minor fork on the right (Wp.5) and a rough track doubling back to the right (Wp.6). A little over a kilometre from the start, we pass the remains of a Moorish hamlet, 30 metres after which we carry straight on at a junction with a narrow concrete track (Wp.7 21M) and enter the **Font de la Mata** *area recreativa* (aka **Font dels Noguers**).

On the far side of the font, we ignore a concrete track climbing to the right and turn left on a lane (Wp.8 23M) leading to the CV714 (Wp.9 1.4km). Carrying straight on along the CV714, we climb toward the main road, passing a minor branch off to our left (Wp.10). At the CV700, we turn right (Wp.11 28M 1.7km), then left 40 metres later (Wp.12), just before the km36 sign, on a

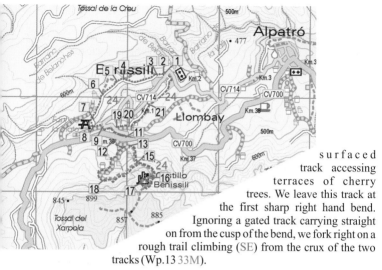

surfaced track accessing terraces of cherry trees. We leave this track at the first sharp right hand bend. Ignoring a gated track carrying straight on from the cusp of the bend, we fork right on a rough trail climbing (SE) from the crux of the two tracks (Wp.13 33M).

Vall de Gallinera

The trail climbs steeply for fifty metres across terraces of cherry trees. On the uppermost terrace, we fork right on a narrow path (Wp.14 36M), still climbing steeply, though the gradient is slightly diminished by the path's serpentine progress.

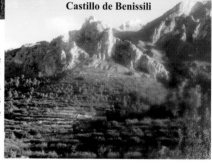

Castillo de Benissili

Reaching a T-junction at the foot of low cliffs (Wp.15 41M), we turn left, enjoying a gentler climb as superb views open out over the **Vall de Gallinera**.

Our route soon bears round to the right and begins zigzagging up to the remains of the castle, passing a well preserved lime kiln en route.

At the time of writing, the two main entrances to the castle are locked while restoration work goes on, but it hardly matters, because the site is so splendid that it would merit a visit even without the ruins.

Just short of the castle we come to a Y-junction (Wp.16 52M). The branch on the right leads to the lower entrance. Rather more interesting, though, is to follow the main path climbing to the left. After passing a roofless outbuilding, we circle round to the south of the castle and the green cabin at its entrance to reach a grassy platform from where there are fine views to the west, notably of **Benicadell** (Wp.17 58M). From here, we can scramble over the rocks behind the green cabin back to the outbuilding and the main path.

Once we've had our fill of this privileged spot, we retrace our steps to Wp.15 (67M), but rather than forking right on the path we climbed, carry straight on for a slightly less precipitous descent. Following a narrow path along the flank of the mountain, we pass a second limekiln just above a cherry orchard, shortly after which the path descends to the right onto an old terrace. At the end of the terrace, we rejoin the main track near the top (Wp.18 76M). Turning right, we follow the track back to Wp.13 and our outward route back to Wp.10 (93M).

Turning right and ignoring a fork on the left (Wp.19) 30 metres later, we fork left 100 metres from the CV714 (Wp.20) on a narrow track that is surfaced for the first 40 metres. At a junction just above km1 of CV714 (Wp.21 100M), we bear right on a path leading to another narrow track, which brings us into **Benissili** on **Carrer de l'Esglesia**. Descending past the church into **Carrer Pont**, we rejoin our outward route at Wp.2.

Probably the best known of the region's limestone arches, **La Forada** above **Benissiva** lends its name to the *sierra* dividing the **Alcala** and **Gallinera** valleys. I can't say it's my favourite example of the phenomenon, but it is big and unquestionably an impressive piece of natural engineering, one that ought to be visited by anyone aspiring to a thorough exploration of the Costa Blanca mountains. Unfortunately, since the devastating fire in 2008, the southern flank of **Serra de la Forada** is not what it used to be. The bright white bulge of the mountain west of **Pena Gros**, which has been stripped of every last vestige of vegetation, serves as a useful landmark from afar, but if you're wandering about up here on a misty day, it all begins to look a bit like something out of Kurosawa's 'Dreams', or even a painting by Paul Nash. For all that, there is a certain stark beauty about the landscape and the views over the **Vall de Gallinera** are very fine.

This is usually treated as a linear route - most people will probably wish to stick with that convention. However, for those who want a few more steps for their pound, I've included a circuit. There's a major drawback, though, to wit, almost four kilometres on the minor road linking the **Alcala** and **Gallinera** valleys. In consequence it's only really recommended in the depths of winter, ideally with a light dusting of snow to smooth the passage. All key junctions on the climb to **La Forada** are marked with new waypoints except at Wp.5.

Linear route to La Forada:

Full circuit:

Access: The walk begins from the twin villages of **Benissiva** and **Benitaia**, which lie between kilometres 43 and 44 of the CV700 in the **Vall de Gallinera**. We park immediately north of the main road in the small square beside **Bar Placeta**, unless it happens to be market day (Thursday), in which case we park on the narrow hard shoulder along the **Benitaia** road, which branches off the CV700 to the south directly opposite the square. In the latter case, continue up the **Benitaia** road on foot to join the walk at Wp.2.

our lane at the start (Wp.1)

Our itinerary starts opposite the **Bar Placeta**, to the right of the bakery (*Forn de Pa*), on a concrete lane, signposted 'Ruta dels 8 Pobles' and 'Forada'(Wp.1 0M). The lane, which is the old road between the two villages and has now been pedestrianized, climbs to **Benitaia**, where we pass the entrance to **Carrer de Dalt**

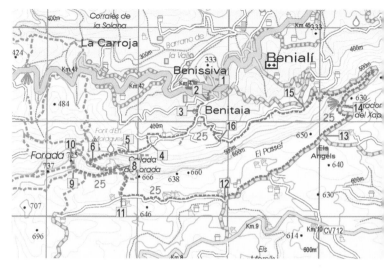

and turn right on a surfaced track (Wp.2 2M). We follow this track for the next 900 metres, climbing past the site of an eighteenth century Franciscan friary (Wp.3) and traversing a succession of immaculately maintained terraces. After passing a cabin apparently sponsored by Castrol (stickers on the door, barrels on the terraces), we cross a stand of pine and wind through a chicane, above which we leave the main track, turning right on a secondary concrete track marked with another 'Forada' waypost (Wp.4 18M). If the waypost happens to disappear, there's a large rock in the angle of the turning painted with faint PR and bright orange waymarks. This is the third turning on the right, not counting entrances to *casetas* and gated tracks accessing terraces.

At a Y-junction 300 metres later, we fork left (Wp.5 24M) on a broad, intermittently paved mule trail, climbing past the **Cova & Font d'En Moragues,** where the trail narrows to a path and we pass the first burned pine. Still climbing steadily, we pass two minor branches off to the right within five metres of one another (Wp.6 35M), after which a broad easterly traverse precedes a series of beautifully made zigzags, where we pass another, cairn-marked path branching off to the right (Wp.7 43M) (a link with alternative routes climbing from **Alpatro** and **La Carroja**). Shortly afterwards, we cross the **Collado de Forada** and enter the fire ravaged terrain of the **Vall d'Alcala,** at which point we leave the PR waymarked path and double back to the right, as indicated by a **Forada** waypost (Wp.8 46M).

Serra de la Forada

Following a stony trail, we pass a tiny roofless ruin, 300 metres after which, a waypost indicates where we leave the main path and cut up to the right (Wp.9 55M). Climbing over bare, cairn-dotted rock, we cross a small retaining wall, beyond which we come to the **Forada** (Wp.10 60M 2.5km). Most people will now

choose to descend by the same route, with the option of following the main path back to Wp.9 rather than clambering over the rocks. For the full circuit, we return to Wp.8 (72M) and turn right. The path to the south crosses rocky terrain then, dipping onto a narrow terrace flanked by broader terraces, heads toward a small whitewashed house beside a ruin. When the path intersects with a Y-junction of two dirt tracks (Wp.11 77M), we turn left along the tail of the Y to pass the whitewashed house and ruin. We follow this track (E) for a little over a kilometre until it joins the **Alcala-Gallinera** road (Wp.12 94M).

Turning left, we climb gently for 1500 metres (NE), after which the road levels out and we pass a turning on the right (Wp.13 111M). 700 metres later, the road winds through a leisurely chicane and passes a track off to the right just before the **Mirador del Xap** (Wp.14 117M). We now descend into the **Vall de Gallinera**, looping round a large green water reservoir, and passing below dramatically streaked cliffs, beyond which the land is cultivated again. 200 metres after passing a small house with a green and red roof, the road goes through a sharp right hand bend and forks into two, one branch descending to **Benissiva**, the other to **Beniali**. Just before the bend, we fork left on a dirt track (Wp.15 137M). We follow this track for a little over a kilometre as it winds along the terraces until it comes to a concreted T-junction (Wp.16 150M), where we turn right to rejoin our outward route at the site of the friary.

I never quite know what to make of the mountains behind **Pego**. It's no accident that the highlands are called the **Pla de Miserat**. You certainly wouldn't want to have to extract a living from this bleak, inhospitable terrain. Yet there's a certain austere grandeur to the landscape, while beauty reveals itself in sudden, unexpected vistas and the sheer drama of the elements, which never seem to be insipid up here, either battering you with withering heat or giving you the old blasted heath treatment as strong winds pile in from higher mountains in the hinterland. Nor is it any accident that **Pego** has one of the most active rambling groups in the region, trail-blazing variants of the **PR58** all over the place, as a result of which it's got more branches than a monkey puzzle tree and is rivalled only by the **PRs 53** and **181** for its tentacular grasp. These people love their mountains dearly; woe betide any visitor who suggests they're a bit, well, dry. In this itinerary, we sample a little of everything, to wit one very obscure path, one very spectacular path and the idyllic **Refugio de la Figuereta**.

The ascent follows an **SL**, the **Travessia de Boloix**, which is a real labour of love for all concerned as it follows a 'path' that doesn't really exist at all and requires good pathfinding skills (not supernatural ones, I found the way with no guide other than the knowledge that it was there, but still, this is an itinerary for those of you who like a challenge), then picks up a branch of the **PR58** to reach the refuge and return to **Pego**. If you don't like the sound of the SL, effectively off path for 400 metres and obscure for the best part of a kilometre, the itinerary can easily be turned into a linear two way ascent via the PR, clear and well waymarked throughout except for one brief stretch between waypoints 18 & 19. If you opt for this, fork right at Wp.4 then carry straight on (the left hand fork) 75 metres later. The turning at Wp.21 is a broad, clearly waymarked trail. It is on the left, 30 metres after a stretch of very rough concrete (the second stretch of concrete after the barrier preventing cars climbing this track), some 250 metres from a small house with a large terrace and tall chimney. When the path levels out at Wp.19, bear right and look for a waymark on the terrace up to your right (Wp.18), after which the route to the refuge is clear and unmistakable.

Given the rough terrain and obscure path, the **Barranc de les Coves** ascent is not recommended if you're walking alone.

Access: As **Pego** is a large town with a complicated one-way system, for simplicity's sake we approach the start from km9.8 of the CV715 immediately south of the town, taking the broad, unnumbered and unnamed road heading inland toward the mountains. This road is 100 metres south of a large, off-white Franciscan monastery and has a tall electricity pylon on its right hand side. Ignoring PR & SL signs on the left 200 metres from the CV715, we carry straight on at the stop sign after 850 metres, then turn left 75 metres later to reach the **Passeig del Calvario** boulevard where there's a mapboard of the **PR58**. The walk starts 1.4 kilometres from the CV715 at the end of **Passeig del Calvario**, where the boulevard dwindles to a single lane road. We park on the right of the road adjacent to the Stations of the Cross

our start beside the calvario (Wp.1)

gateway.

From the end of **Passeig del Calvario** (Wp.1 0M), we walk along the road beside the

the signpost at Wp.2

calvario, behind which we turn left on a concrete track signposted 'Figuereta PR58' (Wp.2). When the main track doubles back to the right after 300 metres (Wp.3 6M), we carry straight on to reach a second signposted junction 50 metres later, at which point we leave the **PR58** and fork left on the green-and-white waymarked *sendero local*, which at this stage is a dirt track (Wp.4).

sculptures at Wp.5

After a steady climb, our track levels out between a wooden hut and a *caseta* with several sculptures in the garden (Wp.5 21M). Ignoring a path climbing to the left, we carry straight on along the remains of the track, which rapidly becomes impassable for vehicles.

A few hundred metres later, the track dwindles to a trail, which leads to a junction at a broad platform ringed with wooden railings above a small dam (Wp.6 28M). The main trail veers left here, but we carry straight on again, as indicated by a waypost and a waymark on the railings, following a narrow path and climbing steadily again.

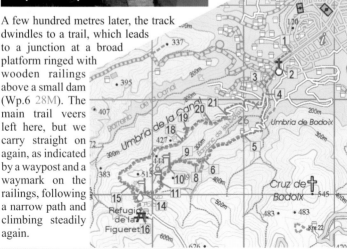

The path crosses some terraces, above which it disappears in scree (Wp.7 33M). This is where the pathfinding problems begin. Bearing left, we climb steadily to steeply along the scree, recovering a very narrow but identifiable path 30 metres later (Wp.8) that bears right, into the more northerly of the two affluents that form **Barranc de les Coves**. Some care is required for the next 100 metres, as the path is eroded in places, after which a better stabilized way traverses another stretch of scree. We climb steadily along the line of the gully, then veer left (Wp.9 41M), at which point the path becomes very steep and virtually invisible. We now climb through a succession of chicanes on an infinitely narrow and very rough way, one that personally I would have given up as a bad idea had it not lead to an SL waypost (Wp.10 47M). From here, we continue climbing in a southwesterly direction, less steeply but no less ruggedly, toward the V at the head of the gully, forty metres before which, the path veers left, obscurely at first but becoming clearer as it climbs to pass three wayposts in quick succession (Wp.11/ Wp.12/ Wp.13 56M). The worst of the pathfinding problems are over!

We now climb across a series of terraces (look for eroded breaches in the retaining walls if in doubt), passing a fifth waypost (Wp.14 59M 3km). Following a steadily improving path, we pass behind an ancient ruin, 75 metres after which we come to a T-junction with the broad, clear path followed by the **Xical** branch of the **PR58** (Wp.15 63M). Turning left, we follow this path up to the **Refugio de la Figuereta** (Wp.16 70M 3.6km), where there are picnic tables, a porch if shelter is required, and a well with a hand pump.

To return to **Pego**, we retrace our steps to Wp.15 (76M) and carry straight on, ignoring a minor fork on the left immediately after the T-junction and a path doubling back to the right 30 metres later (Wp.17).

Following a rough but clear and broad path, we descend toward the most dramatic reaches of **Barranc de la Canal** before veering round to the right (NE). After a brief climb, we cross onto the southern side of the **Xical** spur overlooking **Barranc de les Coves**. Walking alongside a terrace wall, we pass a small ruin, 30 metres after which, our path is blocked by fan palm (Wp.18 94M).

Barranc de la Canal

Dropping onto the terrace below, we maintain a northeasterly direction for 75 metres, approaching a narrow spine of rock protruding from the end of the spur, on the nearside of which, we recover the clear path (Wp.19), which descends below the northern side of the spine of rock. Approaching a dirt track, we ignore a minor path branching off to the left (Wp.20 106M) and carry straight on along the main trail, descending through a stand of pine to join the track lower down (Wp.21 111M). From here, we simply turn right and follow the track all the way back to Wp.4. There is one waymarked shortcut across a bend of the track, but it is badly eroded at the top, so it's easier to stick with the track. We follow the same route from Wp.4 back to the start.

Lumped in with the **Valls de Gallinera**, **Ebo**, **Pop** and **Laguart**, the **Vall de l'Alcala** looks a bit like the poor relation in terms of walking, especially since forest fires laid waste the southern flank of the **Serra de la Forada**. Local sources can be a bit sensitive about this, some material online and in print trying to give the impression that this is the regional capital of *senderismo*. It ain't. The outstanding man-made monument and the most striking natural phenomenon are both best approached from **Vall de Gallinera** (see Walks 24 & 25). But in the right conditions, this valley is still an ideal retreat for ramblers, and I use the word 'ramblers' advisedly. There's no particular place to go, no essential summit or un-missable vista, but if you want somewhere to wander on a windswept winter's day when it would be unwise to be hopping about on some slippery, precipitous summit in high winds, this is the place to be. Ordinarily, I like to pretend the walks I propose are near enough the best possible version of what's on offer. Here that's not the case. This is a lovely walk, but I'm sure there are any number of variants equally as good. This is a landscape designed for just ambling about aimlessly, following your nose, making it up as you go along, trying things out according to whim, urge, energy, and the happenstance of the moment. It's a pure rambling experience.

There's nowhere you run any risks and the worst thing that's likely to happen is that you might have to double back at a dead end. In short, don't go when it's hot or when the conditions are such that the high mountains beckon, but in midwinter, take your time and have a good old nose around the **Vall d'Alcala**. I've never seen it under snow, but I know it happens, I'm sure it must be lovely and, given the network of dirt tracks, neither dangerous nor excessively onerous. The suggested itinerary is all on dirt tracks, most of them drivable, so I wouldn't recommend it at weekends (or on Thursdays during the hunting season), but otherwise the chances are that you'll have the place to yourself.

3 | 3H 15M | 15.3 km | 340m / 340m | | 3

Access: Alcala de la Jovada is at the western end of the CV712, which climbs through the **Valls de Ebo** and **Alcala** from **Pego**. We leave the CV712 at km5.4 (opposite the **Camping La Vall** turning), taking the road into the western end of the village. We park along the unnumbered road that forks right between the playground and the swimming pool, 100 metres from the CV712.

Alcala de la Jovada

From the corner of the road we parked on (Wp.1 0M), we follow **Avinguda Pais Valencia** into the village, passing the swimming pool and bar/restaurant. Crossing the village on a narrow street descending behind a bell tower, we pass a *lavadora*, beyond which we emerge on the eastern edge of the village. Continuing in a northeasterly

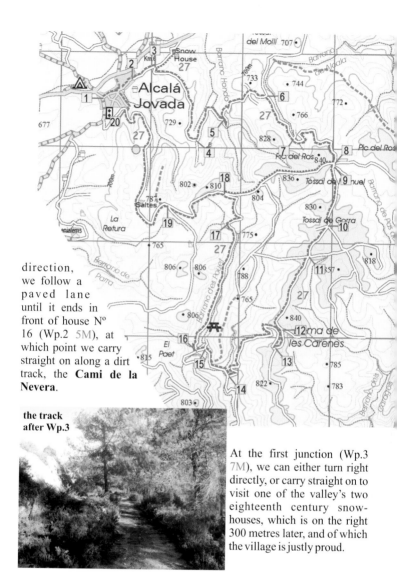

direction, we follow a paved lane until it ends in front of house Nº 16 (Wp.2 5M), at which point we carry straight on along a dirt track, the **Cami de la Nevera**.

the track after Wp.3

At the first junction (Wp.3 7M), we can either turn right directly, or carry straight on to visit one of the valley's two eighteenth century snow-houses, which is on the right 300 metres later, and of which the village is justly proud.

Alternatively, the snow-house is just 50 metres from km6.4 of the CV712 via a signposted track, so you can drive there before or after the main walk. On the assumption that you do choose to visit on foot, I've allowed 15 minutes for the return to Wp.3, where we now turn left, climbing along a narrow track into the sparse woodland to the south.

The track crosses a treeless rise, beyond which we discover a surprisingly convolute landscape. After heading south, we swing round to the left, passing a branch on the right (Wp.4 28M). We then descend into the bed of the **Barranc Hondo** (Wp.5 35M), which we follow to the right for 30 metres until the track climbs above the ravine. A steady climb (less steep than it looked from the other side) takes us past a crossroads with a gated track on the right and a spur leading to beehives on the left, 200 metres after which we reach a T-junction with a broad, well-stabilized track (Wp.6 44M).

Turning right and ignoring a minor branch on the left 500 metres later (Wp.7 51M), we climb toward **Pic del Ros**, the long, shallow backed, thinly wooded rise that was visible through our descent into **Barranc Hondo**. Fine views open out to the northeast, then to the south as we skirt the eastern edge of **Pic del Ros** to reach a crossroads with a very broad dirt track (Wp.8 62M 5km). For a shorter walk, turn right here and follow the broad track until it rejoins the described itinerary at Wp.18, cutting roughly seven kilometres from the total distance. For the full itinerary, we carry straight on, ignoring a fork to the left 40 metres later (Wp.9).

After a little over 1km, the track splinters in three (Wp.10 74M), and we take the middle fork which runs along a broad ridge overlooking **Barranc d'es Pouet**. Carrying straight on at the next junction (Wp.11 83M), we follow the track toward the high sierras of the south, notably the **Serras de Alfaro** and **La Serrella**. At a Y-junction overlooking the **Barranc de Malafi** (see Walk 37), we fork right (Wp.12 94M), continuing along the ridge for another 250 metres to another triple junction, where the nearest branch doubles back to the right and a minor branch forks right after that (Wp.13 97M). We take the branch doubling back to the right for a long gentle descent to a junction with a track from **Tollos**, the lower reaches of which we use briefly in Walk 37 (Wp.14 115M).

Turning right, we follow this track into **Barranc d"s Pouet**, ignoring a rough branch off to the right (Wp.15 121M) and turning right at a T-junction 50 metres further on (Wp.16). We pass the **Es Pouet** *area recreativa* (a spring and a couple of picnic tables) a couple of hundred metres later, climbing so gently that the incline is barely noticeable.

.. attractive little corral (Wp.17) ..

After passing an attractive little corral (Wp.17 142M), the gradient steepens as we trace out two traverses before rejoining the main track we crossed earlier at Wp.8 (Wp.18 150M). Turning left, we simply follow this track almost all the way back to **Alcala de la Jovada**, ignoring all branches, including a major one doubling back to the left (Wp.19 163M).

En route, we pass **Saltes**, the ruins of a moorish hamlet, one of many peppered about the hills hereabouts, the **Vall d'Alcala** (like many places it should be said) claiming to have been the last redoubt of the Moors during the Valencian re-conquest, the resistance of Al-Azraq being commemorated by the Moorish fountainhead in the village square. 40 metres after a sharp right hand bend directly behind the village, we fork right on a grassy path (Wp.20 189M) passing an exquisite little viaduct. The path enters the top of the village and we carry straight on to descend through the main square to rejoin our outward route.

Tucked away in what seems like a valley within a valley, **Vall d'Ebo** is a lovely little lost corner of **Marina Alta**, a kind of Shangri-La were it not for the fact that the surrounding landscape is so arid. The desiccation, however, does not detract from the magic, and there are plenty of walks up here, several of which are sketched out on mapboards at either end of the village. Most are fairly short, nearly all involve a bit of tarmac, but each and every one of them has some lesser or greater secret at its heart, be it the delightful little **Refugio de la Figuereta** (Walk 26), the rock-pools and small falls of **Les Tolls**, or the exceptional wilds of the **Barranc de l'Infern** (touched upon in Walk 31). Although it's a bit of a 'Grand Old Duke of York', marching you up the hill and then straight back down again, the stroll we feature here combines two of the prettiest paths in the area, the beautifully tailored **Travessia del Masset** and the remains of the mule trail that used to link **Vall d'Ebo** with **Pego**. The climb is along a green and white waymarked *sendero local*, the descent via the yellow and white waymarked **PR58**.

Access: Vall d'Ebo lies on the CV712, 11 kilometres from the junction with the CV715 south of **Pego**. From km15.9 of the CV712 at the eastern end of **Vall d'Ebo** village, we take the branch road south of the **Riu d'Ebo** bridge and turn left 50 metres later on a lane marked with fingerposts for the 'PR43', 'PR58', the 'Travessia del Masset', and 'Font d'en Gili'. We park alongside the water treatment plant 400 metres later or, better still, on the rough ground beside the lane 50 metres beyond that, where a concrete ford crosses the river bed.

our start point at Wp.1

From the preferred parking spot (Wp.1 0M), we set off along the concrete ford (N), but DO NOT immediately cross all the way over to the far bank of the river. There used to be a Y-junction at the end of the ford, but the right-hand branch has been washed away. As a consequence, 30 metres from the start, we bear right (E), into the stony bed of the stream, off-path.

A little under 100 metres from the ford, a cairn of white stones between an oleander bush and a bank of brambles indicates the way up onto the remains of the old track (Wp.2 2M), which climbs directly (N) to the CV712 (Wp.3 7M), where we turn right.

A little under 300 metres later, just before the km17 sign, we turn sharp left on a path signposted 'Travessia del Masset' (Wp.4 10M). Following a clear path, we climb across abandoned terraces and traverse a small spur, on the far side

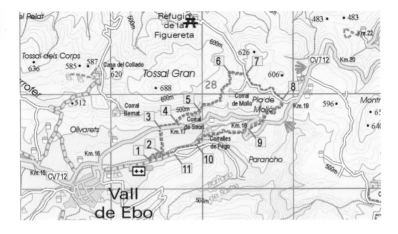

of which we pass the ruins of the **Corral de Saori** and reach the highlight of this itinerary, the **Travessia del Masset** itself, a rough but immaculately plotted path zigzagging up the fractured rock-face of **Tossal Gran** (Wp.5 21M).

The path climbs in easy stages before gradually levelling out and passing a second diminutive ruin, the **Corral de Mollo**. 100 metres later, we come to an oblique Y-junction, immediately to the left of which is a 140 metre deep sinkhole, the **Avenc d'Estret** (Wp.6 37M).

Turning right on the clearer of the two paths, we cross a broad terrace and climb to join the partially surfaced track between the CV712 and the **Refugio de la Figuereta** (Wp.7 40M). If you don't intend doing Walk 26, the refuge is 15 minutes away on the left and well worth a visit, otherwise, we turn right. A little over 500 metres later, we pass a second sinkhole, which looks even more impressive than the **Avenc de Estret**, but which is in fact only 55 metres deep, or so I'm told ... I wasn't down there with my tape measure.

30 metres later (Wp.8 52M), we turn right on the **PR58** for 'Ebo', another attractive, partially cobbled trail that descends to recross the CV712 (Wp.9 60M). After passing the ancient ruins of the **Corrales de Pego**, we veer left, recrossing the **Riu d'Ebo** (Wp.10 73M) to join a track running along the riverbank, at the end of which we recover the access lane (Wp.11) 300 metres from our starting point.

Glance up at the **Serra del Migdia** from the road and it looks decidedly unpromising. "No paths up there," was my first reaction. Occasionally, it's nice to be proven wrong. The mountain is riddled with the things, some among them so very pretty that they deserve considerably more care and publicity than they receive at present. In this short itinerary, we get a taster of the **Serra del Migdia**'s potential and indulge in a brief, mildly hair-raising excursion, scrambling about in the undergrowth looking for a cave with a couple of rather modest Neolithic daubings on the wall.

The diversion to reach the cave won't be to everybody's taste and the reward is rather disappointing if you don't actively enjoy acrobatic antics off the beaten track, but the main loop is exquisite. The vertigo warning applies only to the spur, not the main loop. Given the obscurity of the spur, if you're doing the full thing, best to come accompanied. There are moments on the main loop where thigh-high holm oak obtrudes onto the path, so long trousers are preferable to shorts. If you're not using GPS, you need to be a confident pathfinder.

3 | 2H 06M | 3.75 km | 300m / 300m | ⚠ | ↻ | 🍴 3

Access: The walk starts from **Tormos**, which is on the CV715 between **Orba** and **Pego**. From the southern end of **Tormos** between kilometres 17 and 18 of the CV715, we take **Carrer Pou** into the village centre. Turning left into **Carrer Major** after 100 metres, we pass between the church and *ayuntamiento*, behind which we turn right at a T-junction then almost immediately left to reach the cemetery and *calvary*, parking between the two where the tarmac becomes a dirt track.

Directly behind the first station of the cross, a waymarked rock indicates the start of our itinerary, which is yet another branch of the **PR58** (Wp.1 0M). Following a rocky path (NW), which is intermittently cobbled and stepped, the steps a combination of serendipitous outcrops of rock and tailored stone, we climb into a natural rock garden, dotted with tiny terraces of carob, olive, almond, and pomegranate trees.

starting at Wp.1

Zigzagging up in easy stages, we enter a small pine wood 450 metres from the start, where the path gets slightly rougher, the traverses shorter and occasionally steeper. Towards the top of the wood, the main path swings sharp right along a contour line, but we turn left (W) on a minor path marked by a cairn, then immediately fork right (Wp.2 20M) on a rough trail climbing to a clear path that is also waymarked with old yellow and white PR waymarks. The clear path promptly veers right (N), dwindling to a much narrower path, still occasionally cobbled, but climbing into increasingly wild terrain. As a stone cabin comes into view off to our right, the path swings left, then crosses bare rock waymarked with a bright red dot (Wp.3 33M).

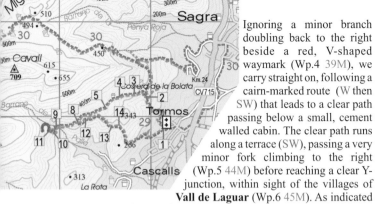

Ignoring a minor branch doubling back to the right beside a red, V-shaped waymark (Wp.4 39M), we carry straight on, following a cairn-marked route (W then SW) that leads to a clear path passing below a small, cement walled cabin. The clear path runs along a terrace (SW), passing a very minor fork climbing to the right (Wp.5 44M) before reaching a clear Y-junction, within sight of the villages of **Vall de Laguar** (Wp.6 45M). As indicated by cairns and waymarks, we fork right on the narrower branch, joining another clear, terrace path less than 10 metres later (Wp.7). Turning left, we descend (50 metres later) across abandoned terraces (watch out for the red waymarks) until a clear path takes us along a terrace to pass a large, waymarked pine tree, where we bear slightly right, climbing across a couple of terraces on a fainter way that leads, after a further 130 metres, to a crossroads waymarked with a large blue dot (Wp.8).

If you've no head for heights or don't care to visit the cave, turn left here. To see the cave paintings, we carry straight on, descending steeply across the rocks (some care required, as the clints are sharp) to a broad, sloping ledge, which we follow down into the **Barranc de la Palla**, on the far side of which, the gated mouth of the cave is clearly visible. Crossing the *barranc* above a dry waterfall (Wp.9 66M), we climb along a narrower but less precipitous ledge, passing tiny retaining walls, above which green and PR waymarks guide us up to the point at which we turn right toward the cave (Wp.10 69M).

cliffs after Wp.12

Following a very rough way, squeezing through the scrub and scrambling over the rocks, we reach the cave 80 metres later (Wp.11 74M). The paintings, such as they are, are on the right. Having peered through the bars (probably with mounting puzzlement), we retrace our steps to Wp.8 (95M) and turn right on the broad path marked by two large cairns.

Forking right 100 metres later (Wp.12), we descend below low cliffs, which nature has decorated rather more delicately than the job done by our ancestors on the cave. Ignoring a minor fork to the right that is 'gated' by two stumpy posts (Wp.13 105M), we contour round the hillside, sticking to the main traces shadowing a retaining wall, then descend across a patch of cobbling to a Y-junction, where there is a blue dot on the wall to our left and a red dash on a rock to our right (Wp.14 107M). Forking right (the traces on the left simply access old terraces), we descend onto a spur overlooking **Tormos**. The path briefly veers right, away from the village, then zigzags down across rough ground, gradually edging north to return to the starting point via the stations of the cross.

30 SENDER DELS POETS

No, don't worry, I'm not going to start waxing lyrical. The poets in question are not verse makers but wells, or little wells to be precise, *pouet* being the diminutive of *pou*. Why the maps and mapboards drop the U, I do not know, but wiser minds than mine, above all wise Catalan minds, agree that we're talking water shafts here, not wordsmiths. I climbed the **Pla dels Poets** with a view to finding a desirable and describable way onto **Monte Cavall**. I failed. But I wasn't disappointed. Instead, I discovered a place of perfect peace and solitude with grand views and some very evocative old stones. If you want peaks and crags and challenges, this is not the walk for you. We do them elsewhere. If you want to get away from it all for a quiet picnic in a lovely lost corner, it is. The path is occasionally obscure, but never worryingly so, and a variety of waymarks (green dots, red dots, yellow and white PR stripes) take turns at confirming the route when it's not obvious. The start of the itinerary is the same as for Walk 29.

| 3 | 2H 40M | 8.55 km | 380m / 380m | ↻ | 3 |

Stroll: the **Tormos-Sagra** loop

Access: The walk starts from **Tormos**, which is on the CV715 between **Orba** and **Pego**. From the southern end of **Tormos** between kilometres 17 and 18 of the CV715, we take **Carrer Pou** into the village centre. Turning left into **Carrer Major** after 100 metres, we pass between the church and *ayuntamiento*, behind which we turn right at a T-junction then almost immediately left to reach the village cemetery and *calvary*, parking between the two where the tarmac becomes a dirt track.

the path above Tormos

Directly behind the first station of the cross, a waymarked rock indicates the start of our path (Wp.1 0M), which climbs into a small pine wood 450 metres later. Towards the top of the wood, we reach a junction (Wp.2 18M), where the present itinerary and Walk 29 diverge.

Ignoring the fainter traces to the left, we turn right, sticking with the main path, which briefly runs along a contour line before climbing gently to a Y-junction (Wp.3 19M). Forking left, as indicated by a large green waymark, we continue climbing gently (NE), bringing the village of **Sagra** into view. Ignoring a minor branch back to the left (Wp.4 24M), we follow a roughly cobbled stretch of path climbing north. Interspersed with brief stretches on the level, gentle climbing continues, bringing us into an affluent of the **Barranc de la Penya Roja** where we pass a signposted junction with a path descending on the right for 'Sagra' (Wp.5 29M). For the stroll, we turn right here, picking up the described itinerary at Wp.12. For the full walk, we carry straight on for

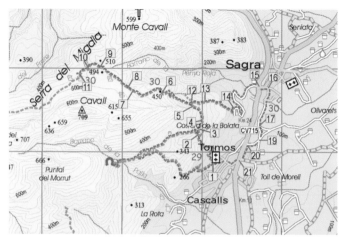

looking east toward Serra de Segaria

'Despoblats', a catchall euphemism usually applied to the hamlets abandoned when the Moors and Moriscos were expelled.

At the top of a series of zigzags, we cross a small pass (Wp.6 44M), beyond which we can just pick out the cross on **Monte Cavall** on the far side of the ravine.

After a brief descent, we resume climbing alongside a line of low cliffs, still following an intermittently cobbled path. Passing a minor fork on the left (Wp.7 54M), we reach the level land of the **Pla dels Poets**, on which we weave through a veritable jungle of fan palm, crossing an outcrop of bare rock (Wp.8 57M), from where we can see the first of the *despoblats* ruins as well as the summits of **Miserat** and **Bodoix**, the latter also topped with a cross.

The path resumes beyond the bare rock, but there are now long stretches where it is almost buried in fan palm, so that the route is invisible except for a few metres immediately in front of us. If in doubt, we head for the ruin, which we pass directly to the right of. 150 metres later, we come to a small col overlooking two more ruins (Wp.9 66M). To the right, PR waymarks indicate an offpath route up to **Monte Cavall**. There also appears to be an equally offpath cairn marked route down into the **Barranc del Penya Roja**. These are describable, but not in the least desirable. I did a couple of hundred metres of the climb, then turned back in disgust. Even the dog looked a bit disgruntled and he'll go anywhere. The **Monte Cavall** route crosses a rough landscape fissured with sharp karstic clints. It's not so much rock hopping as dancing on knives, irregularly serrated knives placed at peculiar angles in such a way that every step is an invitation to a twisted ankle or a broken head. If you really want to get to the top, you will. I didn't.

Instead, we descend to pass to the left of the first ruin (Wp.10 71M), from where a faint path leads to a Y-junction just 30 metres short of the second ruin (Wp.11 74M) bringing **Pego** into view en route.

the homemade sundial

The **PR58** bears left here before swinging round to a more westerly trajectory and descending to the road between the CV712 and **Juves d'Enmig**, but we turn right to visit the ruin, which has a shallow well, the remains of a homemade sundial, and a location so enviable that you can understand all too well why it still shows signs of recent use.

Having enjoyed this privileged spot to the full, we follow the same route back to **Tormos** with the option (recommended) of doing the stroll loop from Wp.5 (112M 5.4km). Turning left here, we descend to a clear junction (Wp.12 113M), where we double back to the right, on a broad, partially cobbled path. A steady descent, winding back and forth as the path twists across terraces, brings us to a slightly obscure stretch 300 metres later, where the clearer traces appear to plunge off the side of the hill over a cataract of terracing (Wp.13 119M). Veering right, we squeeze through a narrow alleyway of shoulder high holm oak, heading directly for **Sagra** (E). After zigzagging down to open, stony ground, we pass a mapboard and follow a broad trail swathed in cistus and heather down to join a dirt track behind **Sagra**'s water hut (Wp.14 130M).

Turning right, we follow the track down to the outskirts of the village, where we carry straight on to cross the CV715 (Wp.15 142M 7km) into a street signposted for the 'CV729'. 100 metres later, we turn right on **Carrer de Tormos** (Wp.16) which leads to a lane, the **Cami de la Bolata**, running parallel with the CV715. When this reaches a Y-junction at the **Bolata** bore hole, we fork left on the **Cami Real** (Wp.17 150M). At the next, inverted Y-junction, we carry straight on (Wp.18), then fork right 50 metres later (Wp.19) on the **Cami de les Hortes**, at the end of which, we turn left (Wp.20 154M). Re-crossing the CV715 in front of the **Bar/Restaurant Tormos** (Wp.21), we take **Carrer Santa Creu** into **Tormos**, at the end of which we turn right into **Carrer Major**, returning to the start as per the access directions.

31 PR147 LA CATEDRAL DEL SENDERISME (BARRANC DE L'INFERN)

For many, **Vall de Laguar** is the capital of Costa Blanca hiking and, along with **Cavall Verd** (Walks 34 & 35), the **PR147** is one of the most celebrated routes in the region, so famous that local hiking groups organize an annual jamboree in which walkers gather from far and wide for a mass jaunt round the mountains, practically queuing on the path in places, before scurrying back to the start for a good feed. The official title is a bit of a misnomer, since we only briefly touch upon the **Barranc de l'Infern**, but when it comes to the nickname, the Cathedral of Hiking, you can see what they're getting at. The natural architecture is grandiose, the collective labour that went into making the '5000 steps' encountered en route might not match the feats of the medieval master masons, but certainly smacks of admirable communal purpose, and if you look at the profile, you'll see that it goes up and down a lot.

The steps are perhaps the most famous feature of the itinerary, 1750 of them down to the **Riu Girona** (who counts these things?), 2050 up to Juves d'Enmig, and a few more thrown in here and there to give a total of 3343 steps up and 2603 down. Laid several centuries ago, they are essentially retaining steps, though some no longer retain an awful lot and its worth watching your step (ouch!) as you descend rather than risking a pratfall in front of the bishop.

some of the many famous steps

The itinerary is well signposted and waymarked throughout, notably at all key intersections, and is easier than a glance at the summary data might suggest. Halfway round, I even found myself wondering whether I'd knock it off before lunch, despite having a picnic with me. I didn't in the end, but bear in mind that, though the climbs necessitate a high exertion rating, the walking is easy throughout, and its a 5-lite. That said, I should point out that the official recommended time for the walk is 6¾ hours! The ravines are nearly always dry, but can be dangerous after or during periods of heavy rain. GPS reception is surprisingly good. The only point at which I experienced poor reception was in the lee of the cliffs towards the end.

Access: The walk starts from the CV721 in **Fleix**, the second of the three **Vall de Laguar** villages (it's sometimes called **Vall de Laguar** el **Poble d'Enmig**), which can be reached via the CV718 from **Orba** or from the CV715 directly north of **Orba**. Follow the CV721 through the village to the junior school (on the right) at its western limit, where there are mapboards for the **PRs 147 & 181** behind a row of stainless steel bins. There is ample parking alongside the school and on the hard shoulder of the CV721.

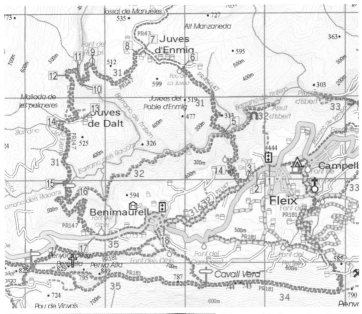

We set off along the CV721 towards **Benimaurell** (Wp.1 0M) and fork right 100 metres later on the old road between the two villages (Wp.2), almost immediately bringing into view the 2050 steps on the far side of the **Riu Girona**. The old road descends to **Font Grossa** and its *lavadero*, 25 metres after which, we leave the road, forking right on a dirt path (Wp.3 4M).

the start point at Wp.1

And that's really all you need to know, as a quick glance at the map will tell you everything else you require for getting to the end.

For the purposes of pacing progress though and to give you an idea of what to expect, soon after leaving the road, the famous 5000 steps begin, rapidly bringing us down to the first of the itinerary's sacred places, the justly famous *forat*, a natural gateway through the rock, the aesthetics of which have been marred somewhat by the installation of a boardwalk to counter erosion (Wp.4 18M).

the boardwalk at Wp.4

We then cross a watercourse below a spectacular cascade, after which the path passes under some ridiculously dramatic cliffs, so over the top (excuse the pun) that they could give a penny dreadful a run for its money in terms of thrills and spills.

No prizes for guessing what awaits us next. No sooner than we hit the bed of the ravine than we bounce right out again (Wp.5 37M 2.2km), the 1750 giving way to the 2050, and we begin our steady haul up to the hamlet of **Juves d'Enmig**. After about a kilometre, the steps become less consistent and are interspersed with patches of dirt path, but there always seems to be one more stairway than you expect, until finally, 1.7km from the river bed, a last long stretch of steps terminates 50 metres from a *caseta*, directly behind which there is a surfaced track and a well, the **Pou de la Juvea**, with a functioning hand pump (Wp.6 70M 3.9km).

Bearing right, we follow the surfaced track up to the hamlet of **Juves d'Enmig**, where the concrete gives way to dirt as we approach a junction with the end of the road linking the hamlet to the CV712. At the junction (Wp.7 78M 4.4km), we turn left for 'Juves de Dalt', then left again at the entrance to a *casa rural* 100 metres later (Wp.8), taking a broad trail that soon dwindles to a terrace path. Beyond the terraces, the cultivated land gives way to scrub and we start descending, superb views opening out over the **Barranc de l'Infern**. After zigzagging down below cliffs, the path (a little perversely) climbs briefly before descending past the **Font del Reinos** (Wp.9 100M) into the bed of the ravine (Wp.10 108M), where the Cathedral Makers do it again - Boing!

100 metres to the right, we climb onto the western flank of the ravine, without benefit of steps this time, on a narrow rocky path (Wp.11 110M). Climbing steadily to steeply for 400 metres, we come to a smooth dirt path following a contour line below terraces (Wp.12 118M), at the end of which we pass a tumbledown cabin, and resume climbing on a gentler gradient, including some stepped sections in case anybody's feeling deprived of their assistance. We zigzag up to a second stretch of terracing and a second traverse (climbing this time), beyond which we reach a signposted junction with a track just above the hamlet of **Juves de Dalt** (Wp.13 131M 7.5km).

Turning right, we climb away from the hamlet to pass a ruin. Immediately after the ruin, we take a signposted path descending to the left alongside the **Barranc del Tuerto** (Wp.14 141M). After crossing the bed of the **Barranc dels Racons** (Wp.15 158M), we pass a branch on the left (Wp.16 163M) (see Walk 32), staying on the main path for **Benimaurell**, still climbing on steps I hope you like steps! After more switchbacks than a fairground full of rides, the path levels out above **Benimaurell** and curves alongside a terrace to join a lane just above **Font del Olbits** (Wp.17 192M 10.8km). The chances are a surfaced road never looked so good. Turning left, we follow the road down to **Benimaurell**, and stick with it as it descends to the left round the outskirts of the village, passing (or possibly not) the **Bar Jalisco** and the **Pub L'Hedrera**, 30 metres after which, we fork left (Wp.18 206M 11.8km) on the old road to **Fleix**, which we follow back to the start of our itinerary.

For those of you who don't like the look of all those ups and downs on the full **Catedral del Senderisme**, but have a head for heights and a taste for getting off the beaten track in wild country, this is the Holy of Holies or, at least, it should be. Funnily enough, this route is little known and rarely appears on maps. Even local ramblers who pride themselves on their passionate love for the **Vall de Laguar** and have been walking here for years, will sheepishly admit that they haven't explored the **Barranc dels Racons**. Quite why is beyond me. It's one of the most spectacular outings on the Costa Blanca, walking up the bed of the broader of the two ravines framed by the **PR147**. Though most of the itinerary coincides with Walk 31, the original bit is so very original that, even if you're familiar with the PR147, you really need to do this walk, too.

Barranc dels Racons

There's a slight risk of vertigo and one or two delicate albeit not wildly dangerous stretches, but with a modicum of care, it's a must do. Must do, but not, for obvious reasons, during or after heavy rain. Access, the start of the walk, and the end are the same as for Walk 31, so I'll keep those bits correspondingly brief and refer you to Walk 31 for more detail.

3   3H 40M   11.5 km   450m   450m   3

Access: See Walk 31

From **Fleix** junior school (Wp.1 0M), we follow the CV721 toward **Benimaurell**, fork right on the old road between the two villages (Wp.2 2M), then right again after **Font Grossa** (Wp.3 5M) onto the 1750 steps down to the **Forat** (Wp.4 21M) and the bed of the **Riu Girona** (Wp.5 44M), at which point the present itinerary and Walk 31 diverge. Our main loop is to the left here, upstream, but I recommend strolling downstream first simply to spend a little more time in this wonderful ravine. How far you go is up to you and the narrows behind the **Presa d'Isbert**, which will put an emphatic stop to your peregrinations.

approachiing Wp.6

We went as far as the diminutive **Assut d'Isbert** reservoir (Wp.6 58M), taking in the improbably perched ruins and breathtaking cliffs below the **Alt de la Mancanera** before returning to Wp.5 (78M).

From Wp.5, we walk upriver, trudging through gravel (gloriously giving underfoot compared to the hard rock that prevails elsewhere) along a wide esplanade for the first few hundred metres, after which the ravine abruptly becomes wilder, obliging us to pick our way across boulders and weave between clumps of oleander before crossing great slabs of bare rock (Wp.7 87M). Thereafter we cross a succession of white wave like rocks, the grooves, curves, fluting and ripcurls of which are so animate that one half expects to see flecks of spindrift curling off their crests. There are intermittent stretches of path along the riverbank, but frankly, the gravel and rocks are more fun. It's pretty wild here and the fact that we've got to find an obscure path in order to get out might seem a little unnerving, but don't worry. First, the ravine will announce quite clearly when we can go no further, secondly, though peculiarly vulnerable due to their situation, there are generally enough cairns and waymarks to indicate the start of the path climbing the southern flank of the ravine. If you're still worried, keep an eye out for the ruins of a small stone cabin on our right about 50 metres above the bed of the river (Wp.8).

400 metres later, as we approach an obvious rise in the riverbed, two cairns on the left frame the start of the narrow path climbing back to the **PR147** (Wp.9 103M). There is also an orange waymark. Climbing steeply, we cross a shoulder cloaked with dwarf fan palm directly in front of the debouchment of **Barranc de l''nfern** (Wp.10 115M). Some care is required in the next 50 metres or so, since the path passes above a thirty metre drop.

We then climb more gently to a second shoulder where fine views open up toward the **Barranc de Cristofol**, an affluent at the head of **Barranc dels Racons** (Wp.11 128M). Veering left (SW), we follow a contour line into a deep gully, at the head of which we cross a watercourse below dry falls (Wp.12 138M). Climbing steadily away from the watercourse, we traverse a hanger of pine, 300 metres after which, we join the PR at a signposted junction (Wp.13 153M).

Time for me to button my lip again. Climbing to the left, we reach the lane above **Benimaurell** (Wp.14 185M), turn left, skirt the village, then fork left 30 metres after the Pub **L'Hedrera** (Wp.15 199M) onto the old road back to our starting point.

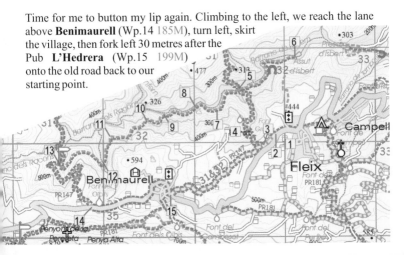

You know how it is when you get one or two celebrated walks in a region, everybody dashing off to make obeisance to the famous beauty spots, leaving lesser known, less striking trails to languish like so many Cinderellas in the shadow of their bigger, brasher siblings. Happily, in this instance, the path makers have applied the 'glass slipper' treatment and plucked a bevy of neglected paths from obscurity to cobble together something very like the Belle of the Ball. The walk doesn't make much sense in the context of the ever proliferating **PR181** (see Walks 34 and 35), of which it is ostensibly a part, but taken as a discrete itinerary exploring the **Vall de Laguar** without straining heart, lung, limb, or nerve (though your liver might take a bit of a beating if you follow the refreshment recommendation a very good house red and a more than palatable house white!), it is an enchanting outing bringing to light all manner of charming nooks and crannies.

The route sounds complicated because there are lots of little paths pieced together, but is actually very easy to follow, being well waymarked and signposted. In fact, all you really need to do is take a cursory glance at the map and get going. Though not essential, a torch is recommended for the tunnel. Also recommended is the excellent **Restaurant La Bruixa de Laguar** (open weekends and bank holidays during the walking season) in the campsite that we pass five minutes from the end.

Access: The walk starts from the CV721 through **Campell**, the first of the three **Vall de Laguar** villages (**el Poble de Baix**), which can be reached via the CV718 from **Orba** or from the CV715 directly north of **Orba**. Arriving in the village, we follow the CV721 through a bottleneck chicane, passing the church, the *carnisseria* and **Forn la Placet**. When the road widens again after the shops, we park in the bays on the left.

the tall waypost at Wp.1

From the parking bays, we retrace our access route, strolling back down the road toward **Orba**, passing to the left of the church to reach the village limits, where we fork on a path that is concreted for the first 50 metres and marked at the top with a tall PR waypost (Wp.1 3M).

A pleasant descent along an ancient, intermittently stepped and cobbled path, which in Autumn is pungent with the ersatz chocolate odour of rotting carob beans, brings us to the end of a dirt track (Wp.2 11M 1km). Following the track to an inverted Y-junction, we bear left (Wp.3 13M), then turn right 25metres later to recover the old path (Wp.4), ten metres along which we reach a signposted junction (Wp.5 15M).

Fontilles is up to our right, but we turn left for **Presa d'Isbert**, descending toward the square scar of a smallholding on the far side of the **Riu Girona** valley, where the livestock have stripped all the vegetation from the hillside. After crossing a carpet of carob beans (so thick it is unlikely to be a seasonal phenomenon), we veer left at a junction with a branch on the right (Wp.6 20M), 50 metres after which, our path joins a dirt track (Wp.7) and we bear left, still descending steadily, to pass behind a large house.

When the dirt track joins a concrete track leading to the large house (Wp.8 25M), we turn left, apparently making a beeline for the garage, but in fact taking a narrow path directly behind the house, which brings us into the bed of the **Barranc de Tamborino** and to the mouth of a tunnel, bored in the late nineteenth century to access the dam construction site (Wp.9 28M 1.7km).

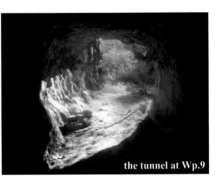

the tunnel at Wp.9

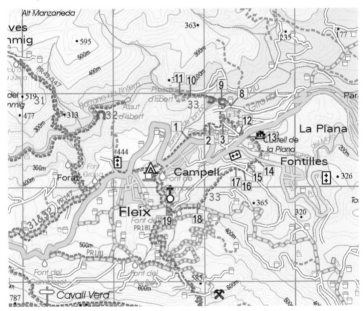

You don't actually need a torch to go through this tunnel, but it helps, since it's about 90 metres long and has a kink in the middle. 100 metres after the tunnel, we fork right (Wp.10), descending into the bed of the river to admire the extraordinary narrows where the **Presa d'Isbert** dam is lodged (Wp.11 36M 2km).

It's possible to loop round the Isbert valley on a lot of tarmac to return to Wp.8, but the tunnel is more fun, so we retrace our steps to Wp.5 and carry straight on for **Fontilles** (60M). The **Fontilles** path runs into a concrete track behind a house at the **Font d'Isbert**.

We follow this track up to the CV721 (Wp.12 66M 3km) where we turn left then right 25 metres later (Wp.13) on a lovely little path contouring round the rocky rise of **Castell de la Plana** before descending into the **Barranc del Moro**, zigzagging across terraces dotted with prickly pear and pomegranates.

prickly pear below Castell de la Plana

After traversing a dry torrent at the bottom of the ravine, we climb an equally twisty and tortuous path before crossing the CV7210 (Wp.14 83M) above the old **Fontilles** sanatorium, now an internationally recognized centre for training medical staff in techniques for combatting leprosy. On the far side of the road, we climb a tailored runoff channel then cross a terrace to climb quite steeply through a pine wood before joining a surfaced track beside a delightful cupola topped cabin (Wp.15 89M).

We bear left here, then double back to the right 50 metres later (Wp.16 92M) on a dirt track. 150 metres along the track, we fork left (Wp.17 94M) and climb gently to a series of terrace paths leading to the **Murla-Fleix** road (Wp.18 105M). We now simply turn right and follow the road back to **Campell**, forking right at the junction 300 metres later (Wp.19) immediately after the **Font dels Gel**. Shortly before arriving back at our starting point, we pass (though not without stopping if we know what's good for us) the **Camping Vall de Laguar Restaurant La Bruixa**.

The ridge dividing the **Valls de Pop** and **Laguar**, the **Serra del Penya**, better known to walkers as **Cavall Verd**, is widely regarded as a classic among Costa Blanca ramblers, and you can see why. Though nothing like as grandiose as the ridges in the hinterland, it's got a distinct, untenanted charm, is readily accessible from the coast, and above all is so immaculately, one's almost tempted to say immoderately, waymarked that it's an ideal introduction to rough, wild, off-path walking for those previously unaccustomed to such antics. It is served by the **PR181**, a hydra like itinerary that keeps springing new branches bearing scant logical affiliation with the ridge apart from a vague proximity. For our exploration of this fine little mountain, we've opted to take two bites at **Cavall Verd**, the present conventional circuit and a western loop, though the two itineraries can easily be combined to make for a longer, full day's outing.

The *sierra's* nickname means 'Green Horse' and dates back to one of the more dismal episodes in Spanish history, the expulsion of the christianized Moriscos in 1609. Driven into the mountains by Phillip III's armies with little more than slingshots and a couple of crossbows with which to defend themselves, the Moriscos came up with the wildly improbable notion that they would be saved by a legendary green horse . . . or a green knight according to some versions. Needless to say, the horse never came, the fugitives were massacred and the survivors deported, but the name stuck.

The route is wild and largely offpath, but not vertiginous, and the only real danger is the bare limestone, burnished by boots and scuffed with dirt, as a consequence of which it can be very slippery when wet. Even on dry days, the exposed rock on the northern slopes can remain damp with dew long into the morning. Recording this itinerary, I nearly came a cropper on at least three separate occasions, and even the dog skidded once. So be warned. Don't do it when it's wet and, even when it seems dry, take very great care indeed.

3	2H 40M	7.6 km	/\	320m		5*
				320m		

*** See Walk 33 for refreshment recommendations**

the PR181 mapboard at Wp.1

Access: The walk starts from the CV721 through **Campell**, the first of the three **Vall de Laguar** villages (el **Poble de Baix**), which can be reached via the CV718 from **Orba** or from the CV715 directly north of **Orba**. Arriving in the village, we follow the CV721 through a bottleneck chicane, passing the church, the *carnisseria* and **Forn la Placet**.

When the road widens again after the shops, we park in the bays on the left. Wp.1 is the **PR181** mapboard, 50 metres beyond the parking bays, where the CV721 bears right and **Carrer de San Antoni** branches off to the left,

signposted 'Restaurant

La Bruixa de Laguar, Camping Vall de Laguar'.

From the mapboard at the intersection of roads (Wp.1 0M), we take **Carrer de San Antoni** on the left, almost immediately bringing **Cavall Verd** into view, including **Penyo Roig**, the large outcrop of rock at its eastern end, which is where our ridge route begins. After passing a pretty *lavadero* and the campsite (restaurant recommended), we climb to the junction with the **Murla-Fleix** road, directly above which a profusion of waymarks indicate a stairway leading to our ongoing path (Wp.2 10M). Forking right at a Y-junction 180 metres later (Wp.3 13M), we cross a broad trail (Wp.4) to join an asphalted spur on a bend of a road (Wp.5 15M). Bearing left, we climb along the road for 400 metres until it splits into two surfaced tracks at the **Casa de los Pinos** (Wp.6 22M). Carrying straight on, we follow the right hand track for 150 metres then climb to the right on a clearly waymarked shortcut (Wp.7 24M). After re-crossing the track 75 metres later (Wp.8) and cutting across a bend, we reach a signposted intersection of itineraries in front of **Caseta de Adolfo** (Wp.9 29M). The lane to the right heads for **Benimaurell**, but we bear left for **Cavall Vert**, turning right on a stony track 50 metres later (Wp.10). Just before the end of the concrete that seals the top of the track, we turn left on a narrow path (Wp.11 32M), climbing steadily amid pine and holm oak to cross the tail end of another dirt track (Wp.12 38M). The climb continues, initially on a broad trail, then on a narrow path, up towards the fissured rock at the western edge of **Penyo Roig**, just beyond which we reach a shallow col overlooking the **Vall de Pop** (Wp.13 46M).

the sign at Wp.14

Turning right, we follow a narrow but well waymarked path onto the ridge, passing to the right of a mini summit 75 metres later to reach our first 'offpath' stretch, traversing bare rock. Our route continues like this, on patches of path, sheets of rock, and occasionally on outcrops of karst, but pathfinding is never a problem, since there is a waymark every fifty metres or so. Again, watch out for wet rocks here, particularly on the northern flank of the ridge. They're absolutely lethal. After a kilometre on the ridge, we pass a metal municipal limit sign (Wp.14 67M) and the ridge becomes rather more dramatic, with two distinct pinnacles rising ahead of us. We descend to the left of the first pinnacle, which resembles the head of the Loch Ness monster from the southern side, before traversing bare rock to return to the crest of the ridge and the second pinnacle, where a rope set in a cleat and an iron step cemented to the rock (Wp.15 75M) help us onto a metre-high ledge (though this could easily be circumvented by traversing the bare sheet of rock immediately below it). After a brief spell on the *umbria*, or the shady side of the mountain, we return to the *solana*, picking our way through rocks, offpath again, to reach a small drop where hands and bottoms may be helpful (Wp.16 83M). The pattern of patches of path, sheets of smooth rock, and stretches of karst resumes as we draw nearer to **Benimaurell**, which has been in sight most of the time, and approach the first of the small summits that stipple the western end of **Cavall Verd**.

views as seen from the west

The intersection of the present itinerary with the western loop is at the foot of this summit, where there is a new signpost, three large cairns, and bright red waymarks as well as the yellow and white stripes of the PR (Wp.17 94M 4.8km). To do the full ridge route, carry straight on here, picking up Walk 35 at Wp.11 and rejoining the present itinerary at Wp.20.

Otherwise, we fork right on the path marked with a red arrow. Excuse the repetition, but yet again, beware of slippery rocks, as we are now descending on the *umbria*, where the dew holds longest. At a patch of rubble behind an ancient retaining wall 250 metres later, the path disappears briefly, but clear waymarks on a rock to our right indicate its continuation (Wp.18 101M), crossing a final sheet of rock. Thereafter, a clear but narrow path zigzags down the **Umbria de Benimaurell**, passing a spring in the lee of the rocks, 50 metres after which it runs into a bend on a partially surfaced track (Wp.19 114M). Bearing right, we descend past a threshing circle, 90 metres after which Walk 35 feeds in from the left (Wp.20 118M).

Carrying straight on into **Benimaurell**, we turn right at the first crossroads on **Carrer de Colon** (Wp.21 121M 5.2km), and descend through the village. Immediately after the third turning on the left, we descend to the left on waymarked steps leading to the old road between **Benimaurell** and **Fleix**, which we follow for the next 1.5km (Wp.22 122M), passing en route the signposted junction where the **PR147** descends into the **Riu Girona** gorge (see Walks 31 & 32) (Wp.23 138M). When the old road joins the CV721 (Wp.24 141M), we carry straight on into **Fleix**, passing two turnings on the right into the centre of the village, after which we fork right in front of the **Bar L'Anoer** (Wp.25 144M). 40 metres later, we carry straight on between *consultori* and **Casa Rural Terranova** (Wp.26), and simply follow the surfaced track between **Fleix** and **Campell** back to our starting point.

When I first visited the **Vall de Laguar**, I was a little puzzled as to why local walkers, particularly expats, seemed to regard **Cavall Verd** as the 'ne plus ultra' of Costa Blanca walking. After doing this walk, I began to understand. It's a wonderfully wild little ridge, the paths are lovely, the offpath walking immaculately waymarked, and the views are breathtaking throughout.

Venta del Collao

As for lunch, that was wonderful, lovely, immaculate and breathtaking all at the same time, the **Venta del Collao** (open Thursdays to Sundays) proving itself the culinary climax of the months spent researching this book, so much so that we went back on the last day to celebrate.

In short, if you only do one bit of **Cavall Verd** during your visit, this is the bit to do; and if you only go to one restaurant during your visit, this is the one to go to.

New waymarks, wayposts, signposts and mapboards appeared on the **PR181** the week before this itinerary was recorded. One reason for this was that several of the old signposts had been ripped up and dumped by the side of the road in places far removed from the actual junctions they originally indicated, so bear in mind that not all the sign and wayposts here might stand the test of time, notably those in the vicinity of roads and houses, where they're readily getatable and/or liable to antagonize.

Access: The starting point is the **Collado de Garga** between **Vall de Pop** and **Vall de Laguar**, on the cusp of the unnumbered road, the **Cami dels Olivarets**, that climbs from the end of the CV721 at **Benimaurell**, the last of the three **Vall de Laguar** villages (**el Poble de Dalt**). The CV721 can be reached via the CV718 from **Orba** or from the CV715 directly north of **Orba**. As you enter **Benimaurell**, take care to turn right for the 'Hotel' (not 'Centre Urba'), then turn left 300 metres later (signposted 'Venta del Collao') at the junction with the road forking right to the hotel, after which you will find yourself on the **Cami dels Olivarets** above **Benimaurell**. The *collado* is a little over 2.5km. There is plenty of parking beside the **Venta del Collao** restaurant on the right of the road and space for two cars in a layby on the left. **NB** En route to the start, a little over 1.5km after leaving **Benimaurell**, we pass Wp.6.

The walk starts on the opposite side of the road from the *venta*, to the left of the metal gates, on a shady, wayposted path burrowing (NE) through holm oak

Vall de Laguar from between Wps.2&3

(Wp.1 0M). At a junction with a concrete track just below a wooden house (Wp.2), we turn right, passing directly behind the house onto a stony path climbing (E) onto the left flank of the **Castellet de Garga** ridge. Immediately, superb views open out over **Barrancs del Racons** and **Infern**, and it pretty much stays that way for the rest of the walk.

At a signposted junction on an unnamed col (Wp.3 9M), we turn sharp left, following a very pretty, partially stepped path descending alongside terraces of almonds. As we near a house just above the **Cami dels Olivarets** lane, the path becomes a rough dirt track, which feeds into a well stabilized track between the house and the road. At the junction of the two tracks directly in front of the house (Wp.4 17M), we turn right, as if to enter the house, then turn left a couple of metres short of the gate on a path descending to the **Cami dels Olivarets**. Turning right on the road (Wp.5), we descend to a lefthand bend 30 metres later, where we again turn right on a wayposted path (Wp.6 20M).

The path follows a contour line, then cuts onto higher ground to run along a very narrow terrace before traversing largely untenanted hillside. We then descend, gently for the most part, to **Benimaurell**, directly behind which we intersect with Walk 34 on a narrow, surfaced track (Wp.7 45M). Turning right and ignoring a track forking left 25 metres later (Wp.8), we climb between terraces of almond and olive until the track doubles back to the right, at which point we

Benimaurell hotel

carry straight on (Wp.9 49M) along a waymarked path. Climbing steadily, we pass a small spring, after which the gradient eases, and a surprisingly elegant stairway leads to a pleasingly serpentine path snaking along the hillside (SE) before doubling back to the right (S) and zigzagging up to cross a broad sheet of bare rock (Wp.10 62M).

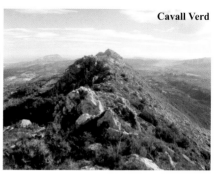

Thereafter, a clear path climbs (SE) to a recently signposted junction on the back of **Cavall Verd** (Wp.11 68M). Turning right, we begin our ridge walk, climbing across bare rock.

The walking on the first stretch of the ridge is off-path, but the way is rarely in doubt, the easiest route being well waymarked, generally following the crest though occasionally favouring faint trodden ways on one flank or the other to avoid clambering directly over a series of small, undistinguished and largely indistinguishable summits. For the purposes of waystaging, we cross the first mini-summit some 300 metres later (Wp.12 79M). The waymarked route drops down onto a trodden way on the northern flank to skirt the next summit, after which we climb a third rise to pass immediately to the right of a solitary holm oak (Wp.13 91M).

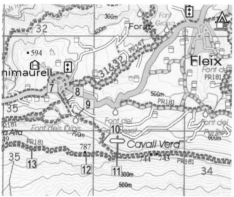

Thereafter, the trodden way becomes an increasingly clear path, descending to the left of the ridge's high point, **Penya Alt**, to enter a hanger of pine (Wp.14 100M).

Emerging from the wood a couple of hundred metres later, we pass below the **Penyons de la Perereta**, the easternmost of which is topped with a cross. Ignoring a clear path doubling back to the right (Wp.15 108M) and a faint branch forking right (Wp.16 112M), we stick to the waymarked path, which brings us back to the crossroads at Wp.3 (115M).

From here, we can turn left to do an additional loop down to **Font de la Mata**, but if you're anything like me, being only 600 metres away from the *venta*, cold beer and a bite to eat will probably seem rather more imperative

Having walked part of the ever proliferating **PR58** the previous day, the singular, slightly stolid title of this walk made me smile 'The Path of Parcent'. It sounds a bit unpromising, as if to say, "That's The Path, that's it, that's your lot, we haven't got any other ones, so you'll just have to make do with what we've got." Factor in the rather bland, smooth aspect of the **Serra del Carrascal de Parcent**, largely devoid of the cliffs, pinnacles and crags that make the Costa Blanca mountains so beguiling, and you might be forgiven for wondering what the appeal is. There's a most spectacular road over this *sierra*. Why put yourself to the trouble of hoofing it? As it happens, there are several reasons. First, appearances are deceptive and there are plenty of startling corners tucked away in the little visited mountains lining the southern side of the **Vall de Pop**. Second, this is a wild landscape in which one gets well off the beaten track (in fact there aren't any for a while) without manifestly putting life and limb at risk. Third, the situation of the **Serra del Carrascal de Parcent** is such that it tempts one to put forward an Argument By Design, to wit that there must be a Supreme Being or else why would this mountain be so perfectly placed for enjoying the fabulous panorama of the loftier, more flamboyant, flashier summits that surround it? If you've got any doubts as to this, all I need to say is that (as with Walk 12) there's a firewatch hut on top and they've always got the best views.

Access: Parcent town is at the intersection of the CV720 from **Pedreguer** and the CV715 between Orba and **Callosa d'en Sarria**. Our itinerary starts from the crossroads at km38.6 of the CV720, two hundred metres east of the CV715. Just west of the crossroads, there is an ad for 'El Casino' and a sign indicating 'Orba 6/Pego 18'. There is plenty of parking on **Avinguda d'Alacant**, the broad road crossing new housing development north of the CV720.

From **Avinguda d'Alacant** (Wp.1 0M), we stroll along the CV720 toward the coast for 130 metres to reach the **Barranquet** lane (on the opposite side of the road just after the **Bodega Parcent**), where we join the waymarked itinerary (Wp.2). Turning right, we follow the lane for 50 metres until it swings left to cross the dry **Barranc de les Cabres** stream (Wp.3), at which point, we descend into

Avinguda d'Alcant (Wp.1)

the Baranquet lane (Wp.2)

the streambed (rather than carrying on along the left bank as the waymarking seems to suggest). At first, the streambed is smoothed by the passage of vehicles accessing a white house on the right bank (our left) 200 metres later, but after that it's a much rougher, boulder strewn watercourse. 100 metres after the white house, as we draw abreast of a large green house on our right, we scramble up to the left onto a dirt track (and it is a scramble, though there's an easier way onto the track 75 metres further along) (Wp.4 11M).

We follow this track along the right bank of the stream until it crosses the CV715 (Wp.5 17M), where we carry straight on along a concrete track. Climbing steadily, we stick with the concrete track until it ends at an attractive cottage (Wp.6 25M), where we again carry straight on, this time on a broad trail, still climbing steadily, passing two branches on the right, the first with another broad trail (Wp.7 35M), the second with a narrow path (Wp.8 39M). 250 metres after the second branch, we reach a T-junction with a well stabilized track (Wp.9 43M). Turning right, we follow the track until it ends at **Font de la Foia** (Wp.10 45M 2.7km).

Waymarks above the font indicate our ongoing route, a narrow path climbing to the southwest. For the next two kilometres, there's no going wrong and no going easy, as we embark on the main climb, slogging up to the **Alts de Polupi**. Crossing a rocky rise after the head of the **Barranc de la Foia**, we ignore a very minor fork off to the right (Wp.11 67M). On the far side of the next fold in the mountain, we pass a pair of iron posts with PR plaques on them, 100 metres after which the path levels out, passing a dry well.

The climbing soon resumes as we again ignore a minor fork off to the right (Wp.12 86M) a couple of hundred metres after the PR plaques. Sticking to the waymarked path as it weaves across a hillside quilted with a pretty patchwork of broom, cistus, oak, heather, and esparto grass, we pass two more PR plaques, the second at a T-junction with a cairn and waymarked route climbing from **Benigembla** (Wp.13 94M) (worth pausing here to admire the wrinkled hide of **Cavall Verd** directly to the north, the snout of which is particularly impressive from this perspective).

Turning left, we pass a fifth plaque 250 metres later,

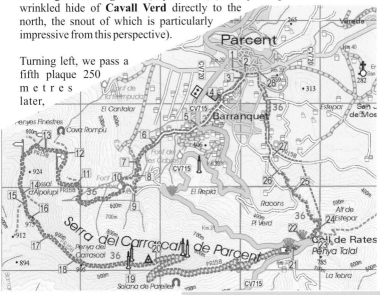

at which point the path levels out and we can see, off to our right, the firewatch hut on **Alts del Cocoll** and, just below it, the faint line of an abandoned airfield. Some care is required here, as the uplands are ribboned with goat tracks and there's a longish stretch with no path to speak of at all.

Alts de Cocoll

Crossing a low rise, we come to an unmarked Y-junction on the nearside of a small conical summit, the **Tossal d'Alpolupi** (Wp.14 110M). Forking right and ignoring a minor fork off to the right 100 metres later (Wp.15), we climb directly over the **Tossal**, bringing into view the *sierras* to the south.

The path effectively disappears here (Wp.16 117M), but progress is not problematic, as we simply stay on the high ground and maintain our southeasterly direction, traversing a pasture peppered with limestone and goats' pellets.

The ridge ahead of us is formed of a series of mini summits. Passing to the left of the next outcrop of rock, still off-path, we pick our way between clints of limestone, sometimes teetering on top of them, to a second barren little pasture, on the left of which (Wp.17 124M), ancient waymarks indicate our ongoing route, favouring the northern flank of the ridge, heading toward two small radio masts. 30 metres later, a faint trodden way resolves itself amid the rock and scrub. You wouldn't want to get too carried away and call this a path, not yet at least, but it is a distinct and, step by step, clear way, either traced out in the stony dirt or scuffed across the rocks by muddy hooves.

Keeping our eyes peeled for the regular waymarks, we continue along the northern flank to reach a small col (Wp.18 133M) just short of a distinct mini-summit, the **Penya del Carrascal**. We stay on the northern side of this summit, though only by a couple of metres, after which we descend to a second col, where the path, which is now clearly visible from a distance, passes onto the southern flank of the ridge. 50 metres short of the masts we saw earlier, waymarks guide us onto a pathless stretch running along the spine of the ridge. We pass just next to the radio masts (Wp.19 147M), after which the clear path resumes, recovering the southern flank to join the end of the concrete track accessing the firewatch hut (Wp.20 153M).

I often complain about the compulsive concreting of mountain tracks on the Costa Blanca, but I must say, this one is most welcome after the rough ridge walking, the more so I would imagine if you haven't brought a picnic and intend eating at the **Coll de Rates** restaurant, which is a couple of kilometres away and is open everyday from midmorning until late afternoon. Strolling down the track enjoying splendid views throughout, we pass (this may take some time) the restaurant and approach the CV715 at **Coll de Rates**.

The mirador

Ten metres short of the road, just before the restaurant sign, we turn left (Wp.21 193M) on an unmarked path descending toward a *mirador*, clearly visible below us on the far side of the road. Crossing the road (Wp.22 196M), we descend to the right of the *mirador* on a broad, badly eroded path.

At a signposted junction with the SL119 which branches off to the right for **Xalo** (Wp.23 201M), we carry straight on, descending to a Y-junction (Wp.24 204M), where we fork left on the **Cami de ses Revoltes,** an ancient, partially cobbled mule trail. You'll soon understand the name. It's so serpentine that you could get whiplash if you came down here too fast. Carrying straight on at a crossroads with a rough track (Wp.25 220M), we stick with the cobbled trail, which eventually broadens to a dirt track behind an orange grove. 40 metres later, we turn left at a T-junction (Wp.26 228M) and descend to a staggered crossroads on the bend of a well stabilized track (Wp.27 231M). Carrying straight on and ignoring the branch off to the left immediately afterwards, we follow this track and the lane it leads into back to the CV720 (Wp.28), where we turn left to return to the start.

One of the happiest walking holidays I have had was spent exploring the fabulously obscure canyons and ravines of central Spain, places so remote and wild that on at least one occasion it took us an entire afternoon to track down a loaf of bread, enquires about the nearest baker eliciting responses that would have seemed more appropriate for rumours about some fabled creature lurking in the distant recesses of the wilderness, one that could only be seen during certain phases of the moon, and even then required the tracking skills of Natty Bumppo and the visual acuity of Hawk Eye. I don't know what they did about breakfast, but toast clearly wasn't on the menu.

The **Barranc de Malafi** is not quite so remote and wild as that, but given the proximity of the densely populated coast, it does a very credible impersonation of a lost corner in a land bereft of inhabitants.

Barranc de Malafi

Add grand views over the surrounding sierras and a rarely visited rockscape blessed with an austere, almost otherworldly beauty, and you have the perfect pretext for strapping on your boots and heading for the hinterland.

The **Barranc de Malafi** is ordinarily traversed as part of the **PR168**, a 30km, two day walk between **Benimassot** and **Castell de Castells**. In order to experience this extraordinary ravine in a single day, we've worked out this interesting route over **Serra l'Alfaro**, the range defining the southern side of the gorge. There's a long stretch on surfaced tracks at the start, but that's no bad thing, as the unsurfaced trails that take us across the top of the *sierra* are very rough underfoot. There's a fair amount of thorny scrub to be pushed through in the ravine, so long trousers are preferable to shorts. Length and the number of intersections dictate a moderately detailed description, but the route is easy to follow, the first stretch being well waymarked, the traverse of the *sierra* very straightforward, and the way through the ravine as obvious as it is obscure! You'll see what I mean on the ground, but basically, despite skimpy paths, there's generally only one way to go when you're in a ravine. **Alfaro** is not recommended on Thursdays and weekends during the hunting season.

4 | 6H | 20.5 km | 530m / 530m | 0

Access: The walk starts from **Pla de Petracos**, a celebrated site of cave paintings midway along the **Vall de Pop** between **Benigembla** and **Castell de Castells**. From km28.1 of the CV720, which connects **Pedreguer** with the hinterland, we take the turning to the north indicated by a brown 'Pla de

Petracos' sign, setting the odometer at zero. We pass Wp.2 at km1.3 then park in the large layby on the left at km1.7, where the new asphalt ends and the road continues as a roughly metalled lane.

From the parking area (Wp.1 0M), we walk back along the road, passing a signpost indicating the way up to the cave paintings at the foot of the cliffs off to our left. 175 metres later, we turn right on the PR signposted path for 'Castell de Castells' (Wp.2 6M). Climbing away from the road, we pass behind a recently restored house, after which the path narrows. 400 metres from the road, we cross a terrace then climb to join a rough dirt track (Wp.3 27M). Turning left and carrying straight on at a crossroads 30 metres later (Wp.4), we climb toward a house, just short of which, at a clearly signposted junction, we fork left on a narrow terrace path strewn with rubble (Wp.5 31M). At the far end of the terrace (Wp.6 34M), we climb (W then SW) on an obscure, but well waymarked path leading to another dirt track (Wp.7 41M). Turning left, we follow this track to a roughly metalled lane climbing from the CV720, which is where our long stretch of road and surfaced track walking begins (Wp.8 50M 1.9km).

Turning right, we follow this lane until it ends a little over two kilometres later, climbing steadily and passing en route the **Font de Espelda** (Wp.9 62M) and a signposted junction where the PR branches left on a terrace path (Wp.10 65M). After leaving the PR, we climb above a small hamlet to reach the end of the asphalt (Wp.11 84M 4km) at a Y-junction with a dirt track on the right and a concrete track on the left.

Forking left, we take the intermittently surfaced track onto the barren lands of **L'Alfaro**. Immediately after passing a well, we ignore a faint branch to the left (Wp.12 98M) and bear right (NW), passing an abandoned corral on the left of the track. If you fancy a break here and want to contemplate the austere scenery from an equally austere seat, there is an ancient wooden chair tucked behind the corral, which should survive another few years exposure to the elements. We then loop round the head of a ravine and climb to a major junction with a concreted branch climbing to the right marked with a dead-end sign (Wp.13 112M 5.9km).

Our track soon veers round to the west, winding across a magnificently desolate landscape, views opening out down toward the sea, over the **Barranc de Malafi**, and north towards the fire ravaged ridge of the **Serra Forada**.

looking north to Serra Forada

It's worth identifying the bleached white hump of the **Serra Forada** because, shortly after that comes into view, we can see a zigzag straight ahead of us (to the west) on the northern flank of **L'Alfaro**.

This zigzag is directly above the point at which we descend into the **Malafi** valley.

the rough track traversing Alfaro

Meandering along the back of **L'Alfaro**, still climbing occasionally, we follow an increasingly rough and stony track, on which the only vehicle you risk seeing is the odd quadbike, and even most of them seem shy of the unstable surface.

After a long, gentle climb, the track levels off within sight of the summit and, off to the left, **Els Frares de Quatretondeta** (see Walk 13) (Wp.14 158M 8.6km). The walking becomes slightly easier underfoot here as we skirt a small plateau and pass to the right of the summit, where superb views open out along the length of the **Malafi** gorge, and the zigzag we spotted earlier comes back into view. After a brief zigzag of our own and a lengthy traverse on rougher ground, we descend steeply through a scree filled gully to a junction at the bottom of the zigzag seen almost five kilometres earlier (Wp.15 203M 11.2km), where we veer right to continue our steady descent.

entering the ravine

After a series of tight spirals, a gentle traverse brings us down to a broad track descending from **Tollos**, at which point we double back to the right, rejoining the **PR168** (Wp.16 219M 12.5km).

The rest of the walk is either clearly waymarked and signposted, or in the bed of the ravine, where you can't really go wrong, but just have to keep ploughing on there's no way out apart from at either end!

We fork right at a Y-junction 700 metres later (Wp.17 228M 13.2km) then again 600 metres after that (Wp.18 237M), the second time leaving the dirt track to follow the increasingly narrow path that runs the length of the ravine.

Hereon in, description is increasingly redundant, as it's simply a question of following the faint stretches of path that crisscross and occasionally run along the dry bed of the ravine. The path generally favours the left bank, but crosses the stream 24 times.

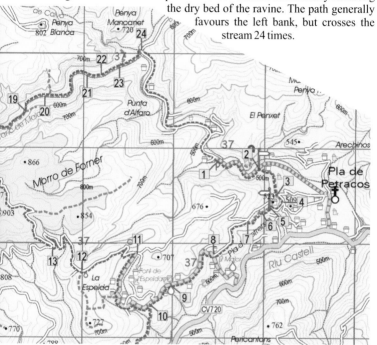

The only point at which the way is not clear comes a little over three kilometres from Wp.18.

After a relatively long stretch in the riverbed, there's a goat path climbing to the right (Wp.19 302M 16.7km). We ignore this and stay in the riverbed for another 250 metres before recovering the waymarked path on the left bank (Wp.20 306M 17km). After another two crossings, a dam wall comes into view and we drop into the riverbed before climbing back onto the left bank, passing immediately to the left of the dam (Wp.21 319M 17.8km). Careful, there's a nasty little foot trap immediately after the dam wall.

Beyond the dam, a good path traverses a terrace of almond trees before dropping back into the wide and, at this stage, bulldozer smoothed bed of the watercourse (Wp.22 18km). 200 metres later, another terrace path on the left (Wp.23 325M) (quite narrow, you might prefer to stay in the riverbed which emerges at the same point) brings us back to the **Pla de Petracos** lane (Wp.24 330M 18.5km). We turn right and follow the lane back to the start.

This glossary contains Spanish and Catalán words found in the text (shown in *italics*), plus other local words that you may encounter.

SPANISH	CATALÁN	
a		
agua, con/sin gas		water, fizzy/still
aljibe	aljub	ancient cistern/reservoir
alto	dalt	high, upper
área recreativa		picnic spot, usually with barbecues, toilets, water
	assut	reservoir/weir
atalaya		ancient watch-tower
avenida	avinguda	avenue
ayuntamiento	ayuntament	town hall
b		
bajo	baix	low
bajo	avall	lower
barranco	barranc	gorge, ravine
	bassa	pond, pool or reservoir
botadores		stone steps in country walls
c		
cala		creek, small bay, sometimes just a tiny coastal indentation
cala		inlet, cove
calle	carrer	street
camino	camí	road, path or way
camino real	camí real	royal road, once a major donkey trail
campo		countryside, field
canaleta	siquia	man-made water channel, including anything from a concrete canal to delicately arched aqueducts
carritx		pampas-like grass
casa	can/ca	house of (as *chez* in French)
casa de nieve	casa neu	snow pit/ice house
caseta		hut, cabin, small house
cingles		cliffs, crags; most often used to describe the sort of short,abrupt cliffs that typically define the rounded summits of many Catalán and Mallorcan mountains
ciudad	ciutat	city
coll		saddle, neck or pass
correos		post office
costa		coast
cumbre		summit
e		
embalse		reservoir
ermita		hermitage, small church, shrine
f		
faro		lighthouse
fiesta		festival, public holiday
finca	lluc	farm
forn de calc	horno de calç	lime kiln
fuente	font	spring, well
l		
lavadero		public laundry area
llano	pla	plain, flat land
m		
medio	mig	middle

mercado	**mercat**	market
mirador		viewing point, sometimes with man-made facilities, more often a natural place with a good view
morro		snout or muzzle, a rounded summit

p

parada		bus stop
particular		private
paseo	**passeig**	walkway
peatones		pedestrians
peña	**penya/penyal**	rock or boulder, used for a knoll or pinnacle on a ridge
pico	**puig**	translates as 'hill' or 'height', though more often a peak or mountain
pista		dirt road
pista forestal		forest road
playa	**platja**	beach
plaza	**plaça**	town square
pozo	**pou**	well
privado		private
prohibido el paso		no entry
puerto	**port**	port, mountain pass

r

refugio		mountain refuge, some offering basic overnight accommodation

s

santo/a	**san/sant**	saint
santuario	**santuari**	monastery, hermitage
sendero	**senda**	footpath, trail
sitja (pl. sitjes)	**sitja**	charcoal burning area or circle
	solana	sunny side of the mountain
su	**son, sa, ses**	his, her, their

t

tipico		typical, locals' café/bar
toro bravo		wild bull
torre		tower, often a coastal watchtower built to warn of approaching pirates, or a Moorish lookout tower
torrente	**torrent**	stream

u

urbanización		housing development
	umbria	shady side of the mountain

The following web links can also be found on our website www.walking.demon.co.uk (go to our Costa Blanca page).

APPENDIX A - USEFUL INFORMATION WEBSITES FOR SERVICES AND SIGHTS IN THE VICINITY OF EACH WALK

There's a wealth of material about Costa Blanca on the web, most of it posted by people trying to sell houses. The following links may help you navigate your way to some of the more useful.

GENERAL WEBSITES:
http://en.comunitatvalenciana.com/home/home-english/493
http://costablanca.angloinfo.com   http://www.alicante-spain.com
http://www.costablancaworld.com   www.eatoutcostablanca.com
http://www.costablancauncovered.comhttp://theolivebranch.net
http://www.destinoguadalest.com   http://www.muntanyadalacant.com

WALK 1 XALO
General Information
http://www.valldepop.es
Accommodation
http://www.hallofromxalo.com   http://www.caseriodelmirador.com
http://www.visitcasadelibertad.com http://www.villaarcoiris.com

WALK 2 POLOP
General Information
http://www.polop.org (Spanish)

WALKS 3 & 4 FINESTRAT
General Information
http://www.ayto-finestrat.es/index.php (Spanish)
Accommodation
http://www.casafigueretes.es   http://theorangehouse.co.uk

WALKS 5 & 6 SELLA
General Information
http://www.sella.es (Spanish)
Accommodation
ww.casaroc.com   http://www.caisaitoni.com
http://www.sellabunkhouse.com   http://www.villapico.com
Alternative activities:
Horse riding   http://www.equushorseriding.com
Rock climbing -
http://theorangehouse.co.uk/rock-climbing-areas/sella
http://www.rockfax.com/databases/results
http://www.rockbusters.net/en/rock-climbing
holidays/courses/trip/coaching/guiding/location/sella-costa-blanca-spain

WALKS 7 & 8 CONFRIDES
General Information
> http://www.abdet.com

Accommodation
> http://www.elpirineoconfrides.com/enhttp://www.racodelsord.com

WALK 9 BENIFATO
General Information
> http://www.benifato.es (Spanish)

Accommodation
> www.elcasalotdebenifato.com

WALKS 10 & 11 BENIMANTELL
General Information
> http://www.benimantell.es (Spanish)

Accommodation
> http://www.ruralguadalest.com   http://www.hostaltrestellador.com

WALK 12 BENASU
General Information
> http://www.benasau.es (Spanish)

WALK 13 QUATRETONDETA
General Information
> http://www.inn-spain.com   http://www.quatretondeta.es
(Spanish)

Accommodation
> http://quatretondeta.com

WALKS 14 - 16 FAGECA & FAMORCA
General Information
> http://www.facheca.es (Spanish)   http://www.famorca.com
> http://www.famorca.es (Spanish)

Accommodation
> http://casaruralfamorca.galeon.com
> http://www.bedandbreakfast-fontdevida.com

WALKS 17 & 18 CASTELL DE CASTELLS
General Information
> http://www.castelldecastells.es (Spanish) http://en.valldepop.es

Accommodation
> http://www.mountainholidays-spain.com/accommodation.htm

WALK 19 TARBENA
General Information
> http://www.tarbena.es (Spanish)

Accommodation
Haven't stayed there myself, but judging by the site (www.la-murta.eu),
the rambler-friendly, English-run La Murta has everything one could hope
for.
> http://www.hotel-tarbena.com   http://www.casalehmi.com
> http://www.cansueno.eu

WALK 20 BOLULLA
General Information
http://www.bolulla.es (Spanish)
Accommodation
http://www.fincapanoramica.com   http://www.finca-el-tossal.com

WALKS 21 & 22 ORXA
General Information
http://www.lorcha.es (Spanish)   http://www.sueno.info/lorcha.htm
Accommodation
http://www.tururac.com/senderismo-patrimonial

WALK 23 VALL DE PLANES
General Information
http://www.ayuntamiento.es/planes
Accommodation
http://www.terrerola.com

WALK 24 & 25 VALL DE GALLINERA
General Information
http://www.valldegallinera.es (Spanish)
Accommodation
http://www.elcaprichodelaportuguesa.com
http://www.casagallinera.es   http://www.sastre-segui.com
WALK 26 PEGO
General Information
http://www.pego.org (Spanish)
Accommodation
http://www.hostalreig.com   http://www.hostalelvea.com
Birdwatching near Pego
http://www.costablancabirdclub.com/Pego

WALK 27 VALL D'ALCALA
General Information
ww.lavalldalcala.es (Spanish)
Accommodation
http://www.casaruralines.es   http://www.fontdalcala.com

WALK 28 VALL D'EBO
General Information
http://www.lavalldebo.org (Catalan)
Accommodation
http://www.lesvicentes.com

WALK 29 & 30 TORMOS
General Information
http://www.tormos.es (Spanish)
Accommodation
See Walks 31 - 35

WALK 31 VALL DE LAGUAR
General Information
http://www.lavalldelaguar.es (Spanish)http://www.valldelaguar.com
Accommodation
http://www.calluis.com   http://www.campinglaguar.com
http://www.hotelalahuar.com   http://www.solterreno.es

WALK 36 PARCENT
General Information
http://en.valldepop.es
Accommodation
http://en.valldepop.es

WALK 37 PLA DE PETRACOS
Accommodation
http://en.valldepop.es

APPENDIX B CYCLING

A lot of work has been done in recent years to promote cycling in the Costa Blanca mountains, including the opening of a dedicated cycling centre in **Orxa** (Walks 21-22).The official website for the centre is:-

http://en.comunitatvalenciana.com/centre-btt-el-comtat/2

which includes links to PDFs detailing nine signposted itineraries. Individuals have also posted GPS records for these routes on the Wikiloc file sharing site:

http://es.wikiloc.com

RUTA 1 - L'ESTRET DE L'INFERN

RUTA 2 - L'ORXA-BENIARRÉS

RUTA 3 - EL CIRCO DE LA SAFOR
RUTA 4 - L'ALBURECA

RUTA 5 - EL BARRANC DE L'ENCANTADA

RUTA 6 - EL BENICADELL

RUTA 7 - LA VALL D'ALBAIDA Y LA SIERRA DE ADOR

RUTA 8 - LA SOLANA DEL BENICADELL

RUTA 9 - LA VALL D'ALCALÀ

More bike routes are available at

http://www.bikemap.net

If these itineraries seem like too much effort (and a lot of them look very strenuous indeed) somebody has come up with the rather brilliant idea of offering downhill cycle rides, details of which can be found at:-

`http://www.thedownhillbikeride.com
http://www.costablanca.org/

APPENDIX C PUBLICATIONS (IN ENGLISH)

Inland Trips from the Costa Blanca
Derek Workman (Author)
Santana Guides [Paperback] (car trips) (1 Nov 2006)
ISBN-13: 978-8489954564

Costa Blanca Walks
Charles Davis (Author)
Santana Guides [Paperback] (1 Mar 2007)
ISBN-13: 978-8489954571

A Birdwatching Guide to Eastern Spain
Malcolm Palmer (Author), John Busby (Illustrator)
Arlequin Press Birdwatching Guides [Paperback] (1 Jun 2001)
ISBN-13: 978-1900159661

Where to Watch Birds in Northern and Eastern Spain
Michael Rebane, Ernest Garcia (Authors)
Christopher Helm Publishers Ltd [Paperback](13 Jun 2008)
ISBN-13: 978-0713683141

Wild Spain: The Animals, Plants and Landscapes *Teresa Farino (Author)*
New Holland Publishers Ltd [Hardcover] (25 Mar 2009)
ISBN-13: 978-1847731265

Valencia and the Costa Blanca
Miles Roddis (Author)
Lonely Planet Regional Guides [Paperback] (1 May 2002)
ISBN-13: 978-1740590327

DK Eyewitness Top 10 Travel Guide: Costa Blanca
Mary-Ann Gallagher (Author)
Dorling Kindersley [Paperback] (1 Jun 2011)
ISBN-13: 978-1405360883

Costa Blanca: Rockclimbing Guide from Rockfax
Chris Craggs, Alan James (Authors)
Rockfax Ltd [Paperback] (31 Jan 2005)
ISBN-13: 978-1873341957

A

Aitana   6, 18, 27, 40, 48-53, 63, 70, 75, 81
Alcala de la Jovada   7, 114, 116
Alcoi   29, 48, 61, 96, 102, 103
Alcoy   51, 95
Algar   91, 92, 94
Alicante   11, 14, 104
Alpatro   101, 105, 109
Alt de la Mancanera   127
Altea   28
Altet de Canonge   57
Alto de Tronca   81
Alts de Polupi   139, 140
Alts del Cocoll   17, 85, 140
Arcs de Castell de Castells   83
Arcs dels Xorquets   93, 94
Aspres de Famorca   76, 77, 81, 82
Assut de Salt   41
Assut d'Isbert   127
Avenc d'Estret   118

B

Baetic Cordillera   11
Bancal del Morro   34, 35, 38
Bar Jalisco   126
Bar Placeta   108
Bar/Rte Tormos   123
Barranc de Bou   71
Barranc de Ginebra   71
Barranc de la Canal   6, 29, 30, 56, 73, 75-77, 81, 94, 113
Barranc de la Canal Negre   93
Barranc de la Carrasca   97
Barranc de la Cova Roja   94
Barranc de la Foia   139
Barranc de la Palla   120
Barranc de la Penya Roja   121
Barranc de l'Encantada   7, 103
Barranc de les Cabres   138
Barranc de les Coves   111, 113
Barranc de les Marietes   32, 33, 36
Barranc de les Viudes   90
Barranc de l'Infern   95, 117, 124, 126, 128, 136, 152
Barranc de Malafi   8, 10, 116, 142, 143
Barranc de Sacanyar   93
Barranc de Sacarest   5, 36, 38, 39
Barranc de Tamborino   130
Barranc de Vessant   96, 97
Barranc del Arc   42, 44, 45, 60
Barranc del Monesillo   72
Barranc del Moro   8, 69, 78, 129, 131
Barranc del Pas   90
Barranc del Pinar   71
Barranc del Salt   57, 59
Barranc del Tuerto   126
Barranc del Xarquer   43, 59
Barranc del Xorquet   94
Barranc dels Bassiets   97
Barranc dels Racons   8, 126-128
Barranc d'es Pouet   116
Barranc Fondo   70
Barranc Hondo   115, 116
Barranca de Gulabdar   31, 39, 58
Bassa de Batle   40, 41
Benasu   6, 61, 149
Beniali   110
Benicadell   97, 102, 104, 107, 152
Benidorm   11, 29, 32, 46, 48, 51, 61
Benifato   6, 47, 51, 53, 149
Benigembla   17, 139, 142
Benimantell   6, 29, 44, 54, 57, 59, 149
Benimaurell   8, 125-128, 133-136
Benissa   26, 89
Benissili   7, 101, 105-107
Benissiva   7, 108, 110
Benitaia   108
Big Wolf   6, 76
Bodoix   122
Bolulla   7, 92, 150

C

Calderes (bridge)   103
Callosa d'en Sarria   27, 29, 39, 56, 88, 92, 94, 138

Calvary	61, 119, 121	Coll de Rates	
Cami de la Font		(restaurant)	141
Roja	66	Coll del Pouet	31, 33, 35, 36, 38, 39
Cami de la		Colladet de	
Rabosa	74, 76, 79	Sardina	86
Cami de les Foies	86, 87	Collado de	
Cami de l'Olivar	68	Benissili	105
Cami de Sanxet	59	Collado de Forada	109
Cami de ses		Collado de Garga	135
Revoltes	141	Collado del Llamp	31, 36, 39
Cami del Carrascal	6, 64, 65	Confrides	6, 18, 46, 48, 49, 55, 62,
Cami del Comte			70-72, 105, 149
Meiral	68, 71	Corral de los	
Cami dels		Senyores	56
Olivarets	135, 136	Corral de Mollo	118
Cami des Clots	6, 64-66	Corral de Saori	118
Campell	8, 129, 131, 132, 134	Corral del Port	55
Camping La Vall	114	Corrales de Pego	118
Cantalar del Gil	72	Cova de Gregori	96
Carrasca de la		Cova del Forat	26, 28
Tia Sofia	66	Cova d'en	
Carrascal de		Moragues	109
Parcent	18, 88, 138	Cova Foradada	67
Casa Lehmi (hotel)	89	Cuatro Vientos	57
Casa Martin	100	Cullera	102
Casa Rural		Cumbre de Aitana	6, 48, 51, 70
Masanet	68	Cumbre de Aixorta	6, 83-85
Casa Rural		**E**	
Terranova	134	El Castellet	6, 56, 77, 80-84
Cases de Bernia	26	El Morer	59
Castell de Castells	4, 6, 17, 18, 68, 73, 80,	El Portell	32
	81, 83, 87, 94, 142, 143	El Recingle Alt	6, 56, 61
Castell de		El Regall	6, 56, 76, 78
Confrides	6, 18, 46, 55	El Salt	104
Castell de Garx	92-94	Els Arcs	6, 11, 83, 86, 87, 94
Castell de la Plana	131	Els Castellets	36-39, 43
Castell de la		Els Frares	6, 61, 62, 144
Serrella	80	Els Frares de	
Castellet de Castell		Quatrerondeta	144
de Castells	80	Embalse de	
Castellet de Garga	136	Beniarres	103
Castillo de Alcala	105	Era del Rallat	81
Castillo de		Es Pouet	7, 114, 116
Benissili	7, 105, 106	**F**	
Cava de la Safor	98	Facheca	68, 149
Cavall Verd	4, 8, 10, 124, 132, 133,	Fageca	6, 64, 68, 70, 149
	135, 137, 139	Famorca	4, 69, 73, 75-77, 81, 82,
Centre BTT El			149
Comtat	101, 152	Finca de la Llum	100
Cerro de los		Finestrat	5, 31, 32, 35, 36, 44, 59,
Parados	56, 77, 85		148
Cim de la Safor	7, 101, 102	Fleix	8, 124, 126, 127, 131,
Circ de la Safor	95, 101		133, 134
Clot del Moli	104	Foia de Font Major	85
Clot del Noguer	73-75, 78, 79	Foia del Sabaig	89
Coll de Borrell	68, 72	Foia Roja	43
Coll de la Caseta		Font de	
del Rector	62	Benissalim	89
Coll de l'Orenga	27	Font de Espelda	143

Font de Forata 49, 50, 53
Font de la Foia 139
Font de la Mata 105, 137
Font de l'Acantara 40, 42, 43
Font de l'Anouer 53
Font de l'Arbre 6, 48
Font de l'Arc 43
Font de Moli Area
  Recreativa 54
Font de Partagat 6, 51, 53, 56
Font de Serra 72
Font del Cuquero 68, 69
Font del Espinal 66
Font del Moli 31, 32, 35, 36, 54
Font del Noguer 75, 79
Font del Olbits 126
Font del Reinos 126
Font dels Bassiets 96, 97
Font dels dos
  Xorros 64
Font dels Gel 131
Font dels Noguers 105
Font dels Olbis 7, 88, 90
Font dels Teix 94
Font dels Teixos 84-86
Font d'en
  Moragues 109
Font Grossa 125, 127
Font Roja 66, 67, 70
Fontilles 130, 131
Forat 127
Fort de Bernia 26, 27

G
Gorga 64, 68
Guadalest 29, 39, 46, 82, 84, 148,
  149

H
Hierbas
  (restaurant) 80, 83

I
Isidor 45

J
Juves de Dalt 126
Juves d'Enmig 123, 124, 126

L
La Bruixa de
  Laguar
  (restaurant) 129, 131, 133
La Carroja 109
La Catedral del
  Senderisme 8, 124, 127
La Cova de Bernat 68, 69
La Finestra de la
  Safor 99
La Forada 7, 18, 108, 109, 114
La Planissa 33
La Ruta del Aigua 5, 40
La Serrella 56, 61, 68, 80, 116

Les Bardals 71
Les Tolls 117
Les Valls 17
Little Wolf 4, 6, 73
Llombai 12, 101

M
Malafi 8, 10, 116, 142-144
Mallada del Llop 6, 56, 73, 76-78
Marina Alta 117
Mas de l'Oficial 37
Mas de Sacarest 38, 39
Maset del
  Secretari 43
Mirador del Xap 110
Miserat 122
Moli de la
  Encantada 104
Monte Cavall 121, 122
Monte Ponoch 31
Monte Ponoig 5, 29, 35, 36, 38, 39, 56
Morro Blau 83, 85, 93
Morro de la
  Campana 27
Morro de Modesto 54
Muro de Alcoi 103
Nevera de la Safor 98
Orba 119, 121, 124, 129, 132,
  135, 138
Orxa 7, 95, 96, 100, 101, 104,
  150

P
Parcent 8, 13, 18, 56, 88, 138,
  151
Parelles 7, 88
Partagat 6, 47, 51, 53, 56
Pas de la Rabosa 48-53
Pas del
  Comptador 44, 45, 57, 60, 71
Pas Tancat 94
Passet de la
  Rabosa 36-38
Passet del Golero 43-45, 59
Pedreguer 64, 68, 73, 80, 83, 138,
  142
Pego 7, 103, 111, 113, 114,
  117-119, 121, 123, 138,
  150
Pena Gros 108
Penya Alta 52, 62, 85
Penya de Sella 40, 42
Penya del
  Carrascal 140
Penya Escoda 86, 87
Penyo Cabal 35, 38, 39
Penyo Mulero 6, 45, 54, 55
Penyo Roc 60
Penyo Roig 133
Penyons de la
  Perereta 137

Penyot de l'Orenga	27
Perputxent	100
Pic de Serrella	76
Pic del Ros	116
Pla de la Casa	6, 56, 67, 68, 70-72, 78
Pla de la Salvia	62
Pla de Miserat	111
Pla de Petracos	8, 142, 145, 151
Pla de Petracos	8, 142, 145
Pla dels Poets	121, 122
Poble d'Enmig	124
Polop	5, 18, 29-33, 36, 38, 57, 148
Port de Confrides	62, 70, 71
Port de Tagarina	51, 52
Port de Tudons	48
Portet de Castells	82, 84
Pou de la Juvea	126
Pou de Neu	68
Pou del Frare	81
Pouet d'en Campos	70
PR 7	5, 26-28
PR 9	44, 45, 60
PR 10	51, 56
PR 12	32, 37, 38, 39, 43, 44, 59
PR 13	31, 32, 33, 38
PR 15	38, 39, 58, 59
PR 17	31, 38, 39
PR 18	82, 84, 85
PR 19	82
PR 20	49
PR 21	51, 56
PR 22	48
PR 23	61, 66, 70-72
PR 24	61, 66, 70, 71
PR 42	95, 97, 100
PR 43	101, 107
PR 44	46
PR 49	94
PR 53	111
PR 58	111-113, 117-119, 123, 138
PR145	7, 88
PR147	8, 124, 127, 128, 134
PR149	6, 80
PR150	82, 84, 85
PR151	83, 86, 87, 94
PR158	8, 138
PR168	69, 73, 142, 144
PR181	111, 129, 132, 135
PR182	6, 68, 70, 72
PR198	40, 42
PR199	40
PR207	97
PR289	32, 33, 35, 36, 38
Presa d'Isbert	8, 127, 130, 131
Pub L'Hedrera	126, 128
Puig Campana	4, 5, 29, 31-33, 36, 38, 40, 43, 55, 56
Q	
Quatretondeta	61, 64, 66, 144, 149
R	
Raco de la Segaissa	27
Raco de les Tovaines	58
Raco del Duc	7, 12, 95, 96, 100
Raco Roig	7, 92, 93
Recingle Alt	6, 56, 61, 63, 78
Recingle Finestra	71
Refugio de la Figuereta	7, 111, 113, 117, 118
Rincon de Pepe (restaurant)	57
Riu d'Arc	42
Riu de les Voltes	41
Riu d'Ebo	117, 118
Riu Girona	124, 125, 127, 130, 134
Riu Sella	41
Riu Serpis	95, 96, 98, 100
Riu Seta	65
Runar de la Mona	40
Ruta de Josep Mascarell	95
Ruta de los Fuentes	95
Ruta del Aigua	5, 40
S	
Sacanyar	86, 93
Sagra	121, 123
Saltes	116
Sanxet	59
Sella	5, 13, 32, 37, 39-44, 51, 59
Sender de Parcent	8, 138
Sender dels Pintors	7, 119
Sender dels Poets	7, 121
Serra de Aixorta	17, 56, 83, 92
Serra de Bernia	5, 26, 39, 56, 62, 84
Serra del Carrascal de Parcent	18, 88, 138
Serra del Ferrer	88
Serra del Migdia	17, 119
Serra del Raco Roig	92
Serra Forada	83, 143
Serra Forada	83, 143
Serra la Safor	7, 95
Serra l'Alfaro	8, 81, 116, 142
Serrals	7, 88, 91
Sierra de Aitana	75
Sierra de Aixorta	60
Sirventa Living Art Gallery	44, 59

SL112   5, 40

T

Tajo de Roldan   32, 35, 43

Tarbena   7, 80, 83, 87, 88, 91, 92, 149

Tormos   7, 17, 119-121, 123, 150

Torre de Dalt   57, 58

Tossal d'Alpolupi   140

Tossal d'Avella   35

Tossal Gran   118

Travessia de Boloix   111

Travessia del Masset   7, 117, 118

U

Umbria de Benimaurell   134

V

Valencia   14, 54, 104, 105, 116, 148

Vall d'Alcala   7, 18, 109, 114, 116

Vall de Gallinera   7, 12, 96, 101, 105, 106, 108, 110, 114, 150

Vall de Guadalest   51, 60

Vall de Laguar   4, 8, 120, 124, 127, 129, 131-133, 135, 136, 151

Vall de Planes   7, 103, 150

Vall de Pop   8, 17, 80, 83, 133, 135, 138, 142

Vall de Seta   63, 70

Vall d'Ebo   7, 18, 114, 117, 118

Venta del Collao   135

Villa Font Freda   46, 47

Villa Monica   104

Villa Nieve   89

Villajoyosa   40, 43

Villalonga   96, 101, 102

Vipas (restaurant)   57

X

Xalo   5, 26, 141

Xarquer   5, 6, 43, 57, 59

Xirles   58